Brooke Larson

Pleasing Tree

 Arc Pair Press

ISBN-13: 978-1-7339719-1-1

"*Pleasing Tree* is a natural history of Larson's vagrancies: guiding YoungWalkers in the Sonoran wilderness, drinking an Amazonian psychotropic herb on Rockaway Beach, falling in love with a dewdrop above Salt Lake City, pissing in the canyons between the buildings in Manhattan, or walking with an Armenian-Palestinian in Jerusalem's Christian Quarter. While there are stories here, Larson never allows them to unfold in a straight line. Instead they ramble like her footprints—a crooked braid. Experience as viewed through lattices, the branches of a tree or the reticulations of the cultures she's adopted. Her language tumbles like a creek, dances like a flute player. Words conjoin and re-conjoin, kinky: facial beehive, piss alchemy, pan-species foreplay, sopping bloodknot, twilit bullshit. This frolic across landscapes, cityscapes, and inscapes is purposeful play, exploring desert blandness and urban loneliness, seasonal affective disorder and communion with plants, the plight of Palestinians and of lovers, the science of stomach bacteria and the mysticism of light and water. As she writes, 'The world is obscene with meaning.'"

~ John Bennion, author of *Falling toward Heaven* and *An Unarmed Woman*

"*Pleasing Tree* is a wakeful series of interdisciplinary excavations into how the human being, when out of options, begins to heal. Into the narrative of a troubled teen trekking into the desert with the ANASAZI wilderness program and then returning, as an adult, to work as a guide herself, Brooke Larson weaves meditations on Native American and Mormon spirituality, the benefits of blandness, the fullness of desert emptiness, the bodily experience of spiritual hunger, and the dangers of over-pathologizing ourselves and each other. With sources spanning biblical myth and botany, Emily Dickinson and John Cage, these essays speak up in favor of the wonderful weirdness inherent in the natural world and in the human being. Larson's prose is large-hearted and trippy, self-aware and funny, expansive and raw. And, ultimately, driven by hope."

~ Jessie van Eerden, author of *My Radio Radio* and *The Long Weeping*

"Brooke Larson's *Pleasing Tree* is a unique hybrid, braiding the personal and the informational, the lyric and the technical, into a series of histories about Mormons and seasonal affective disorder and the desert and the city, but maybe even more importantly, about people, vulnerable, lost, searching in every quadrant of the world for a place to belong."

~ Dustin Parsons, author of *Exploded View: Essays of Fatherhood with Diagrams*

"*Pleasing Tree* is a pilgrimage through landscape and thought, an ecstatic meandering most beautifully wrought, visionary in its wandering. In this deft collection of essays branching with the largess of cellular star stuff, Larson's writing jolts so expansive it becomes difficult to see the world without a shimmering awareness mystifyingly close."

~ Rebbecca Brown, author of *They Become Her* and *Mouth Trap*

Table of Contents

Pleasing Tree

E c o l o g y   o f   A b s e n c e

For starters, the desert is not empty. Things grow in ways you could not dream up. In the Arizona desert, where I was dropped off as a pain-in-the-ass teen, there are ocotillo and prickly pear and yucca and all manner of cactus; creosote bushes and mesquite trees with long, knuckly beans; scads of devil's claw; crucifixion thorns and resurrection plants.

The desert is not unbroken expanse. In the desert there are more things vertical than flat: red canyon walls, mesas and buttes, hoodoos and cairns and geo-acrobatic arches. Not least, the trees. Black walnut, velvet ash and ironwood, oak, alder, Mexican elder, jade-skinned palo verde smooth as scars, and crusty alligator juniper. Why am I surprised? In the heart of nowhere there is always the faint pulse of a seed.

+

Wilderness therapy was a happy accident of Stone Age technology. Effective treatment, a side effect. The intent had been to teach college students primitive survival skills, not life skills, but the fact was young adults were coming home from the middle of nowhere more alive than they'd ever been. The survivalists and their desert experiment couldn't stay off the map forever. Already a host of psychologists and sociologists had picked up on their little prehistoric operation. Everything must evolve, the survivalists knew. And so it was that the ANASAZI Foundation, the first wilderness therapy program, organically, collaboratively, came to be. Precarious kids, following guides through the wilderness, would bushwhack their way forward, all the while cutting new synaptic pathways. They called it ANASAZI after the "Ancient Ones," so named by the Navajo who once inhabited the land on which the teenaged ones tread. Others would come to call it "Treehab."

+

It was 1962. A group of 30 Brigham Young University students, as part of an academic experiment, were dropped off in the Utah desert with a can of peaches each. They would trek across the blister-red terrain to a pick-up van waiting on the other side, one month away. They would have one guide: a young professor, rangy, enthusiastic, and helpless without his thick bottle glasses. Larry Olson's obsession with Native American cultures had lured him into great wastelands as a young boy living in Idaho. He minutely emulated their tools and skills. He became a sophisticate at primitivity. The University had him bring it to the classroom. On meeting him for the first time before the trek, one student recalls thinking, "This skinny white man is gonna get us killed."

The student was Ezekiel Sanchez, a first-generation college kid of migrant workers, and recently expelled from the University. Indeed, all the students were ex-students. Kicked out for chronic failing. Only those with nothing left to lose would agree to be guinea pigs without even the shelter of a lab. The deal: the students would be readmitted to BYU if they spent their summer participating in Larry Olson's raw-brained Stone Age scheme. Ezekiel, back home in Texas hammering once again at the railroad, was fasting when he got the letter of odd invitation. Without the heart to break it to his parents that he would not be returning to school in the fall, Ezekiel had decided to go without food or water until he got a miracle. And so it was. Probation in the wilderness struck him as manna from heaven. He set out for Nowhere, Utah.

Things went south fast in the desert. One guide, and too many lost kids. Olson feared he'd made a fatal mistake. People were starved, injured, sick, falling behind and straying sideways. But then there was Ezekiel. He knew things. Olson had watched him hang back from the group and quietly gather from the land what he needed. Ezekiel's family had long survived like this. One night, sleepless with anxiety, Olson woke Ezekiel and asked for his help leading the group. Ezekiel said he would think about it.

The next day Ezekiel stepped into being a guide, and a month later, the group arrived at their destination. As the story is told, all of the students of the experiment would go on to successfully graduate from the University. Except for one. Ezekiel dropped out of BYU—to accept a position on its faculty. Together he and Larry Olson pioneered a wilderness program and philosophy—the groundwork of what would become a lifelong partnership.

As it became clear that wilderness sojourns were doing something good to people's brains, Olson and Ezekiel found themselves in a forest of eager experts. Experts from psychology, sociology, psychiatry, juvenile justice, family counseling, education, and a slew of other professions—all wanting to analyze and give suggestions on how to enhance the "primitive experience." Through trial and error the survivalists sifted through the mass of ideas and methods. They began to find that the more structured or "contrived" experiences often weakened the impact for participants. It seemed that the more hands-off they were about the hands-on wilderness experience, the more positive the results. "Ultimately, when we founded ANASAZI Foundation," Olson and Ezekiel explained in 1990, "we opted in favor of the original, down-to-earth walking daily—in and with the simple realities of nature." In the Navajo tradition, life is called a "walking." ANASAZI named its approach The Making of a Walking.

+

Desert reminds me of a pubescent body. The puckering place where spare warps to bounty: beauty of earthly awkwardness. Angular, flat planes abruptly interrupted by hard outcrops, jutted ribs of rock and sudden softnesses, lonely globules and lanky pinnacles, every inch sloping, curving, filling, outing, all casting oddish shadows. And then there are the sudden shocks of shrubs. Tufts of trees and scratchy patches. You investigate at twilight. How do all these weird growths fit together? What does this place want to be?

+

When I hike into Girls Band I see the matted beehive of auburn hair. It has risen like nut-gnarled bread since I last saw Rebecca two weeks ago. As I get closer I see twigs sticking out. When she sees who her TrailWalker is she yells, jumps up to hug me, we nearly topple. She shows me her bug bites and brightly tells me a squirrel stole the billionth comb we've given her.

You would think she and I were pals by this welcome. I'm always amazed and amused by how even a short time shifts things radically around out here. Not half a moon ago this girl was threatening to kill me with a ridiculously small rock. I met Rebecca when I was called in as emergency support when she dropped her pack and booked it for a dirt road. I wish she had booked it. She mostly trudged in five- minute intervals and we sat exposed under the July sun, midday, in the dust. Because Rebecca did not have her pack, I did not have mine, as TrailWalkers are not to have more than the YoungWalkers. This meant I was out my long-sleeve shirt and white scarf, making my face and arms a flesh pile for the bugs to swarm. The gnats caught in the zipper of my eyelashes and tickled up my nostrils and in my ears. When I cracked open an eye to look at the New Jersey girl stubbornly slumped on the dirt next to me, I was appalled to see the bugs had no taste for her. She could sit there all day, and she did.

I know the other two girls as well, Jen and Marian. They are older in years and ANASAZI time than Rebecca. This will be their fourth week—three more to go, if the plan doesn't change. The plan often changes. These girls only just met Rebecca, who has been a bit too hostile to join the group till now. Of course this is not the explanation we give the girls. We simply say that Rebecca has been on "walkabout." ANASAZI uses a "romantic language," as Ezekiel calls it. He and his wife, who grew up on the Navajo reservation nearby, have crafted a vocabulary in which imagination chases out negative jargon. Rebecca is not a serious case of oppositional defiant disorder; she's just having her own Walking.

Jen and Marian talk excitedly about all the things we have to do this week, like the freaky moon dance we made up, and sewing sexy moccasins.

"And we're beating the boys to Final D," Jen crows.

I don't tell them that we won't. We definitely won't. Rebecca's dreaded beehive will be a magic hat of tricks for us this week. I have no idea what will come out of it, but it will likely bite.

+

At first blush, the desert appears to be monotone variations on a theme: lack. I don't know that John Cage spent any time in Arizona, but when he took his seat at the piano before an expectant audience, and played—nothing—this was a movement in desert major. The man sat limpid for a small eternity. The audience got restless, whispery, self-conscious, then noisy. Here is where the key shifted in their brains, and they heard themselves: the audience's response *was* the score. The desert is not lack, it is response to lack. It is you hearing yourself.

Desert and speaking are inextricable in Ancient Hebrew, that wilderness tongue, where they share the same root. You can hear the echoes: *midbar/medaber.* They tell of some innate relationship between the barren, empty, silent, and speaking, language, creativity. Nothing so wants to be filled as silence. The quiet of the desert, going way back, is the beginning of speaking and listening.

People go to the wilderness to hear something. Many people say they do. They call it their inner voice, or their god, or the wind, or the void. ANASAZI calls it the One Who Stands Within.

+

Lack itself signals consciousness. How can something be absent apart from our expectations? Absence is a presence of mind. Henri Bergson said that there are no negatives in nature. A negative description is positively our invention. And so it is that loss and absence, inseparable from our awareness, keep us coming to our senses. They activate us. A person recognizes what is lost and sets out to recover it.

Wilderness makes you all kinds of conscious. Everywhere you look is a lack caught in the headlights of your memories: tap water and ice cubes and shampoo and mom's chili chicken casserole and a car and roads to drive it on with no aim but to roll down the windows and turn up the music—oh man—music. The kids sit around the fire and incant lists like magic spells. Napping with your cat; green grapes; down comforters; your sister's laugh when she's hyper; your Dad making pot roast on Sunday afternoon. More than a torturous mantra, it's a fine tuning of awareness. Brooding is one thing, dwelling another. The desert mind dwells between two worlds, perceiving "the nothing that is not there and the nothing that is."

Lack is generative. When the musician doesn't play, the audience crescendos.

+

Blandness is a positive quality, Chinese aesthetics would have it. The bland is a full achievement: not the lack of flavor, but the possibility of all flavors. In the colorless, toneless, soundless, inhere all colors, tones, sounds. It's that temporary moment of loaded indeterminacy: life that has not yet been sacrificed on the altar of particularity: compost of correspondences breaking down to continuities.

The bland longing is not for what has been, but for what has not come into being. The opposite of nostalgia, the bland longs to lose what is particular. It is in the green as it is in the decayed; never in the golden. The bud and mud, not the flower, are the point.

Blandness. The dull is your oyster knife.

+

Our first day hiking we come upon campers. We're lucky that this happens rarely—people aren't exactly flocking to the hell-fired wilderness for a weekend getaway. When a tent does crop up, TrailWalkers go into hyper-alert mode. With Rebecca in this group, me and Gabe, my partner TrailWalker, go nearly ninja. Reflexively we jump to put our bodies between the barbecuers and the girls. In case a YoungWalker makes to hitch a ride with a passing camper or cowboy, we wear a laminated badge on a string around our dirty necks to certify that we are not, in fact, homeless bums who kidnap children.

Rebecca starts hollering and clapping commands—sweetly. Thank God—it's the dog she wants. The mutt wags its tail and starts towards us. I don't think the campers, veiled as they are by palatial bug nets, have seen us. The dog hesitates. All the girls are slapping their thighs now, cooing and kissing. Come on good boy, almost there...

He sniffs the air around us and stops dead in his tracks. You can hear the snort of displeasure as he turns from us and heads back to camp. "Man, even the dogs think we stink," Marian says.

The desert is a vast defamiliarizer: grass, trees, water, plastics, colors, cars, dogs, and most radically, people, shed their invisible everyday skins, pop like hallucinations. When the backdrop is emptiness, every appearance is a burning bush. I remember that as a YoungWalker, a month deep into the solitude of the desert, bumping into a group of campers fairly blew my mind. You are people! Like I am a person! And we see each other! For the first time in my life I felt what might be called *kinship*. I loved the strangers, because they were humans. I couldn't fathom that not long before I had walked through whole crowds of people— real life people!—without so much as looking at them. Didn't I know what they were? People are too incredibly improbable to overlook. Too impossibly incredible.

And all of us being here: way, way too out of this world not to laugh out loud.

+

No place knows more about water than the desert. Its every line and contour, plant and animal, has been sculpted by water, its absence as much as its presence. Lack is its own intimate ecosystem.

I think of desert as the gourmet of water. A glutton will eat without pausing to taste. A gourmet, however, savors not only the meal but the world organized around it—the smells and sounds and placings and pairings, the spaces, lingerings and aftermaths. The desert is a lean muscle toned to taste. A hard tongue that sucks itself dry, plumbing subtleties of wet.

When water itself doesn't do all the talking, you can catch revealing details about it. There are telling trees in the Arizona desert. A cluster of sycamore is a signal of water, present, or soon to return. Cottonwoods are another inside source. They crowd in rings. Once among them, look around. If there's a breeze, I would look up, too: a skyfull of silver leaves ashimmering and shaking. That rustling sound, a susurrus in full sway, is blood buzzing behind the temples, or a conch shell cupped over every pore where every pore is a tiny ear. Trees are vascular graffiti saying *Water was here*.

+

Lack knows more about desire than pleasure physically can. Where pleasure silences desire, lack interrogates it. Pleasure, like all good stories, has a clear beginning and end. Desire is not a good story. It is a dialogue which undermines itself indefinitely. Desire, like the desert, is a skilled curator of lack. It exploits empty space; it is permutational in the extreme. Desire, as long as it lives, evolves. And it can live long, on nothing. In the wilderness desire lives like a Methuselah. Like a Moses, who saw but did not enter the promised land. Desire shows us bittersweet things.

The kids who come to the desert know many things about pleasure but next to nothing about desire. I am one of them, which keeps me coming back to the desert. I want to be a student of desire. I want lack. But not as an end in itself. As a student also of pleasure, I am interested in the way hunger flavors my fill. How contrast cooks with what it has and doesn't have—to make something fresh.

My greatest desire is to not be used to anything. Here is where lack and desire kiss.

Several TrailWalkers adapt ANASAZI as a physical lifestyle to follow on and off the Trail. While I admire this, it is not my way. There is no pleasure in the world like a gruesome grease binge after a week of barely salted lentils. Even as I appreciate stepping off the tracks of high-speed wish fulfillment, I'm already looking forward to hopping back on. With one subtlety: I know I'd be fine if someday I came home to nothing instead of something.

Larry Olson wrote a classic field book, *Outdoor Survival Skills*, that we pack around with us on the Trail. I remember reading the prologue as a 15-year-old and coming up short at one of the traits of a "survivor": a life centered away from comfort and ease. In terms of survival, Olson said, comfort only gets in the way. This odd idea gripped me. What would happen if comfort was no longer a factor in my decisions? What would I do, where would I go? I realized the answer would be: anything and anywhere. If I weren't afraid of discomfort, what would I fear? I couldn't think of one thing. I knew I had in my hands powerful medicine.

+

The desert was the death and rebirth of Mormons. Starting in the east, they made their winding way to the sparsely inhabited wilderness of the west. The tales of persecution, trial and tribulation are religiously recounted, and commemorated every year by Mormons on Pioneer Day. The parades and lawn barbecues, fireworks and pool parties don't do the desert justice. Now in Salt Lake City you can hardly see the desert for the trees.

But when the Mormons first rolled up with their dingy wooden carts and undiminished vision of Zion, all the eye could see was a salty blank wasteland.

Who can say what the heart saw. Who knows, but the godforsaken has got some fearsome godly glow. As the story's told, the prophet Brigham Young, shortly after the Saints' exile from Illinois, was shown in vision a place where the Latter-day Saints would settle and "make the desert blossom like a rose." Months later when Young was confronted with Utah's vast emptiness, he could already point to the exact spot where the Temple would go. Zion was a precognition and an ever after re-cognition, because Zion is nowhere to be seen. And so it came to pass that the rundown prophet leading the half-dead group could look out over the middle of nowhere and pronounce it, legendarily, "the right place."

"His plainspoken direction," says *Our Heritage*, "helped the Saints imagine the possibilities of their new home." Desert is the topography of tragic optimism. And the God of Abraham, the patron of such topography, wrote the tragic optimist's field guide: "Wilderness and the dry land shall be glad, the desert shall rejoice and blossom; like the crocus it shall blossom abundantly." How well this god knows us. Man can't resist irrigating absence.

+

Aiding prophetic fulfillment are the plants themselves, who miraculously outlast the desert's scarce supplies. Dormancy is a gift of the spirit. Oh to unmanifest, to lie low in possibilities. *Euxerophytes*, they're called. *True dry plants*. In the desert these plants can live as if dead for years, decades. Plants in spirit. Just add water, the body will rise.

+

Water is a purely acquired taste. You might say: the acquiring is the taste. There is a story told of a sage who set out to taste the water of all the different springs of the world. He was curious to know the best flavor of all waters. He gave first place to the river of Zhongling, which he found bland at first, but judged gradually to be the best flavor in the world, with which no food can compare. Water is the flavor of sagehood. To taste the richness of the bland is less a matter of receiving a flavor than infusing one: "The sage flavors the flavorless."

Poor, tired sage traveling the world to compare the forgettable. He must have been very thirsty, with fat fingers and a reeling head, by the time he got to the river of Zhongling and acquired a taste. The flavor of water does not exist independent of insight into its worth.

+

Your ankle's swollen? You see black spots? You have stomach cramps and a leg rash and, oops, you've cut off your finger tip. Whatever your ailment, the prescription is the same: Drink More Water. Funny, infuriating, and bogusly effective, Drink More Water is good medicine on ego as well as body. There's nothing that tests a prideful leper like being told to wash in the river.

ANASAZI's go-to nurse—a stunning octogenarian who still kills it in high-heels and turquoise jewelry—never stops telling us: dehydration is the root of all ills. This seems fair, especially from a great-grandmother who can hike to her patients. Dehydration is not unique to the desert. The majority of us are chronically dehydrated, we just don't know it. It's too easy to drown out our thirst with superficial fixes that run on medicated empty. The desert doesn't drain us so much as bring our dry spots to the surface. The sun will have you feel it. But more than we're getting hammered, we're already hungover. The past catches up with you out here.

+

The first time I met Jen I jumped back a little. She is a beautiful girl. But when we met her eyes were so swollen that they deformed the bridge of her nose, her whole face pocked with black scabs and green ooze. Gnat bites. They are brutal. We had all been hit hard—summer brought a freak swarm—but none like Jen. Her arms were more scab than skin.

This is not a 16-year old cheerleader's vision of summer. But Jen is a blend of sweet and tough that makes her persevere politely. She carries her load; she keeps a controlled smile. She doesn't complain.

But now, in front of me, Jen stops hiking. The group halts and turns to her. Jen is scratching her arms off. Now she is crying. Now sobbing, holding her face. She is moaning, shaking. Saying over and over, "I can't do this anymore. Home, I want home."

Everyone knows how she feels, and no one knows what to do. We softly say anything. Our words sound painfully off key. We lower them to a mumble, all but lip-synch the breeze, then fall silent. We stand dumbly around Jen as she cries.

Here is one of the hardest parts of the job for me: seeing my agonized younger self, and being powerless to make her believe in me. She will hike through this and past the worst of adolescence. But in this moment, it is the end of the world for Jen. And I can't be her savior.

The best anyone can do is drink more water.

I take off my bandana and empty my canteen onto it. I lift one of Jen's arms and begin rubbing it down with the cool water. Jen sniffles and lifts her other arm like a sleepy child who wants to be undressed for bed. I bathe it down to the wrist, and at the back of her neck, and behind her ears. I don't talk; water is smoother than I am.

Gabe asks Jen if she wants to hike with the bandana. She slowly nods yes. We re-wet it, drape it around her neck. As we set off down the dry creek bed, a ground swell of feeling rocks me. Wonder at water's power to underwhelm.

+

Whatever is not fully externalized worries you into worrying it. You rub, pick, dig, turn, the indefinite possibilities deepening in your mind. In this way, absence leaves something leftover. Something hidden within for later development. Absence does not leave us.

Chinese aesthetics expresses this quality as a "lingering." Whether it's a tune, a poem, a landscape—holding back initiates overflow.

+

You would think parched land would fling open its doors at the slightest knock of rain. But just the opposite is true. To begin with, most of the desert surface is exposed rock—not particularly absorbent. What surface soil there is expands when wet, essentially sealing off lower layers from needed moisture. The water that does manage to percolate has another problem to deal with: extremely dry soil is difficult to wet. So what's a good rain to do? Much of the water moves across the surface and headlong down slopes. It collects in arroyos. In times of heavy rain, this runoff can create a flood rushing through the arroyo. Rivers! Now-you-see-em, now-you-don't! We call these flash floods, and we take them very seriously when hiking in the summer. What sounds like a climatic magic trick is actually the number one cause of weather-related death. A torrent of water carrying debris and trees and boulders, rushing at you top-speed on your moments-before dry trail, could saw you in half and end the show there.

The desert can move as fast as it can slow, as wet as it can dry. Not a few groups have lost all their gear to a flash flood. And some of us have had to cling to rocks or branches. But no one has ever gone the way of the flood. In its thirty-some years, there has never been a death at ANASAZI. Ezekiel, when he first arrived to the desert in the creation stages, got to his knees and blessed the land for the people who would walk on it. The walking and kneeling has yet to cease.

The desert landscape is protean to the core. Dryness creates runoff, and runoff a flood of possibilities. With the kaleidoscopic flux of surfaces, desert plants and animals evolutionarily shift in turn. All that lack makes for dynamic overflow.

How then is desert life sustained? Internal logic. While the soil of the desert may look pale and dead, the rocks and sand are actually nursing life. Desert pavement—the desert's top layer of close-fitting stones, like Inca craftsmanship—protects the underlying soil from wind erosion. Protection also exists between sand grains, where there is a live lacework of cyanobacteria. These photosynthetic bacteria interlace hands to hold soil particles in place. The desert is a survivor. But it digs in its heels below the surface.

+

Rebecca is not going to hike today. She informs us of this after the group spends five hours packing up, downing lentils, killing our fire, no-tracing our camp, planning our route, and, at last, setting off down the ravine. We exhale all that stale air. The mood lightens. How fresh it feels to be moving, to create a however small breeze between us. Fifteen minutes in, Rebecca throws her pack and plops down.

"Whatcha doin'?" Gabe goes for casual.

"This is stupid. I'm not hiking."

"Well, what do you want to do?"

"Stay here."

Gabe patiently explains that here we have no water, and no flat ground to make camp.

Rebecca also explains herself clearly: "So."

Marian kicks a rock and Jen tears up. This is the second day Rebecca has refused to hike. They turn to look at me, pitiful. As if I could regulate. But part of ANASAZI's empowerment is equal helplessness. In the desert you can't demand. Only appeal.

An hour later, Rebecca relents enough to backtrack the handful of turf to our starting point. The site is along the dry creek and the dry creek is at the base of a shale and cactus mountain.

The girls don't know yet that we are going to go up then down this mountain, and then another one. Gabe and I don't know yet how this will happen. When we take out the maps again, look over what's ahead, we laugh and wipe our foreheads. From here the mountain is an inside joke of indeterminate punch line.

The girls aren't amused. "Ok, who wants to make the fire we put out?"

+

According to the aesthetic of blandness, what a flavor, tone, or landscape lacks in body, it gains in spiritual presence. The art of the bland is less interested in sating the palate than in leading a person to gain a feeling for the Way. Music is divided into two camps: "One that dazzles the senses and one that awakens consciousness." This is the age-old tension. François Jullien, in his book *In Praise of Blandness*, points out that whereas Chinese culture has the myth of silent music, we in the West have the Sirens. Our yearning is for overwhelmed bodily organs.

The desert is not a Siren. It does not dazzle or seduce or bathe itself perennially. The desert is a low, primal growl you discover to be your own stomach. You come to know your hunger; you learn to feed yourself. Indulgence is nowhere in ear shot.

In the desert, you observe, sounds are chewed with the mouth closed.

+

Blandness is the bread and butter of Mormons. I did not say "tea and jam" because Mormons do not drink dark teas. "Strong drinks," such as alcohol and coffee, are prohibited. Our church services, like our beverage selection, are prescriptively bland. We don't have paid ministry, so the Church is run by lay members, untrained in the ways of charismatic preaching. Our sermons, which we do not call sermons but "talks," are to be plain and straightforward. We sing a little, rock some organ.

Instruments with a "prominent or less worshipful sound," like percussion or brass or an acoustic guitar (for heaven's sake!), are, according to the Church Handbook, inappropriate. Our church buildings are unadorned. You will not find a cross or altar anywhere. Men have cropped hair and hairless faces; women wear capped-sleeves and below-kneecap skirts. These church meetings are three hours long, for toddlers and teenagers alike. Here is where our Olympic training in understimulation begins. The air is rarefied, the clock is inching up the mount. Our butt muscles ache.

We do not pepper our speech with strong language. We do not have sex—or anything like unto it—before marriage. Our Temples seem secretive, and are indeed exclusive, but serve most often as a very clean space for an afternoon nap. We're given to shapeless white robes. Our tastes are textureless. Utah has an official State Dessert, and it is jello.

Worship and entertainment have different goals. It would seem Mormon living is boring by design. For it is by boredom that we divine the Holy Spirit, who was not, after all, in the wind, or an earthquake, or a fire, but a still, small voice.

+

I say "we" when I say Mormons. I am not Mormon, but I was raised Mormon, and I consider myself an "ethnic Mormon." People on both sides, Mormons and non-Mormons, find this term ridiculous. It is! But I needed a new term. And laughable seems better than polarized. I have left Mormonism, so I can't say I am Mormon. Yet, if I say I am not Mormon, that ignores my ancestral history and the immersive, idiosyncratic culture that shaped me growing up. To say I am "a cultural Mormon" doesn't work either, because I choose to live outside of that culture. Why not "ex-Mormon?" Succinct enough, except that then I'd also have to add "respectfully-ex-Mormon with a continued appreciation for the religious histories of my family." Enter "ethnic Mormon." I don't want to be Mormon or ex-Mormon, but inhabit the blander state between.

+

Ezekiel and his wife, Pauline, are Native American, and Mormon. There is nothing exotic about this. Mormons and Indians go way back. Mormonism is often called the American religion, and this is true in more than one sense. The Church was not merely founded in America, but its foundation, *The Book of Mormon*, proclaims to be a record of ancient Americans: their origin, civilization, laws, prophets, progress, downfall and destruction. According to *The Book of Mormon*, Native Americans are literal descendants of Abraham. This imbued Mormons with a singular view of Indians in the early 19th-century: they were neither the noble savages of literature nor the sub-human brutes of frontier lore. They were technically God's chosen people. In the 1830s, as the U.S. government passed the Indian Removal Act to push eastern tribes to the western territories, Joseph Smith was proclaiming this land the Native American's God-given birthright.

Joseph Smith wasted no time in meeting with Native Chiefs and telling them so. This did not sit well with the settlers battling Indians for land. It wasn't long before the Mormons, pushed out by the same mobs and Congress, followed their tribal brethren to the empty promises of the wide-open west. From the beginning, Smith saw the establishing of Zion in the wilderness as inseparable from gathering the "lost tribe" of American Indians.

The Book of Mormon is a strange love letter to America's native. It pleads, it reveals, it evades, it threatens and despairs and dares to hope. It makes impossible promises. The title page of the book states that it is "written to the Lamanites, who are a remnant of the House of Israel." The Lamanites were the sometimes righteous, mostly iniquitous people from whom Mormons believe Native Americans, particularly the Navajo, are descended. Some Church leaders have used the terms "Lamanite" and "Navajo" interchangeably, which would kind of be like calling an African a Caininite. In recent years, the

Church has advocated for using the quaintly more PC term "children of Lehi" in place of Lamanite. To be a child of Lehi in the Church has special status. Once, touring the roof of the Church Conference Center in Salt Lake City, Ezekiel Sanchez's face popped out at me from sculpted bronze.

+

Though Mormons have spread out over the world, native interest has never let up. BYU offers programs to learn Navajo as a second language. Selections of *The Book of Mormon* have been translated into Navajo, and, as early as the 1980s, audio translations of talks by Church leaders have been available. In Snowflake, Arizona—a Mormon colony co-founded by my ancestor William Flake, and the dot on the map that makes me related to half the Mormons in Arizona—the Mormon Temple offers its holy services in Navajo. Over 50% of Navajo County, Arizona, is Mormon.

The relationship is not always brotherly. Sharing land, even if it is a wilderness, always breeds complications. To this the good book testifies: tribes split a house as they share it. Across Utah and Arizona, Nevada and Idaho, Mormons and Native Americans overcome and overstep boundaries. One southeastern Utah county, uncomfortably encompassing a rundown Navajo reservation and wealthy Mormon community, has been caught in a storm of lawsuits around racism and inequity. The Navajo and Mormons say they pray for each other, in their peyote ceremonies and sacrament meetings, respectively.

Just north of our ANASAZI stomping ground is the small town, and largest community of the Navajo Nation, Tuba City. The name honors Tuuvi, a Hopi chief who converted to Mormonism in 1870. He invited the Mormons to come settle nearby, and the Navajo and Paiute Indians followed to be near the town's natural springs.

The Navajo used a different name for Tuba City, Tó Naneesdizí. *Tangled waters*. Of course. The place where crosscurrents knot together.

+

"In order for a character to be centered and harmonious," wrote Liu Shao in his treatise on personal aptitudes, "it must be plain, bland, and flavorless. This type of character is thus able to coordinate the five aptitudes and adapt smoothly to all situations." Only the watery can move with the changing contours of a situation. Ideals become insipid: not goal-driven, but goal-diffused. This bland character, rather than push a situation in a given direction, exploits it by catching its groove.

At the heart of versatility is a great pumping flatness.

+

It's unnerving to be so far off our hiking goals. This is a relatively easy week, if you're going by the maps, but we're going by humans. Humans have outrageous elevations. When a thing is very steep, it no longer appears on the map as concentric squiggles: it conflates into a single line. It can't be read. Vertical reality is impossible to map out. You just have to set out.

Human relationships are very vertical climbs. Thick tangled lines where anything can await you.

"Powwow time," says Gabe. His tense face makes it clear. He and I go off a bit from the girls, still in our sights, but not in our face, and we're already breathing easier. TrailWalkers must "powwow" daily to counsel about the Band and go over topographical maps, which the kids cannot see. This is the official powwow. But behind the map curtain, is the wowpow. Expletive venting. Which only wants to laugh. Adolescents in the desert say and do the damnedest things. If Gabe and I didn't take time to endear ourselves to chaos, chaos would kick our heads in.

James tells me how Rebecca was bragging to the other girls that she knows all about plants because she eats at Subway like every day.

We break down into giggles.

"Hey what are you guys doing over there?" The kids get jealous.

"Checking maps," Gabe and I yell back in unison.

"How far are we?" they whine.

"Closer than we've ever been."

Wowpows are essential in remembering that we're not *actually* concerned about failing to make it to our Final Destination. What is Final D, really? Yes, we need to get there so the kids can get food, letters, see their counselors, and most importantly, so Gabe and I can get the hell out of here. But if we didn't get there—what? Somehow everyone makes it home, eventually. Final D is just a key for chaos to play in. A point on the map, but never the point.

ANASAZI considers itself a microcosm of the "wilderness of life." The experience, singular as it feels, is densely fractal. The idea is that the trajectory of one's Walking in the desert mirrors the course of one's life. A movement towards reconciliation, home, and a happiness expansive enough to contain unhappiness. As rooted in the physical as life at ANASAZI is, every action has an almost knee-jerk abstraction. Hiking, making fires, learning plants, building shelters, rationing food, finding water, following tracks, burying poop—all these resonate at a near allegorical frequency. Experiences bounce between the inescapably physical and the playfully detached. Goals are real, but not. The stakes are high, but blink, and they're low. Nowhere do I get more caught up in the realness of the moment, or swept away to a more remote distance. I am stressed out and tuned out, totally invested and ultimately indifferent. I am sharply bland.

My parents tell me that they could, in a matter of seconds, make me do or not do anything as a child by beginning to Count To Ten. I never tested them past Seven, and they never had to come up with the meaning of Ten. I think of each day at ANASAZI as a parent Counting To Ten. It's useful to act like there's a Ten, and freeing to know there's not. Oh, the genius and grace of arbitrary urgency.

Outside the desert it is far harder to hear the bluff in life's numbers.

+

ANASAZI has tried to distance itself as much as possible from popular boot camp philosophy. People are often perplexed that I can do this job without being a trained counselor. I'm even less equipped than that—anything I did know of psychology, ANASAZI's training disabused me of. Its push is away from theory, models, and fixed techniques. The aim is simply to maintain an ancient primitive lifestyle. There are certified therapists who trek out to the desert once a week to meet with the kids, and they are emphatically not called therapists, which word Ezekiel likes to break down as the-rapist. They are called Shadows, which they essentially are, as they follow the experience of the kids and parents far more than they lead it. Nature is given space to do its thing.

The criteria to work at ANASAZI is almost entirely devoid of credentials. It's a character contract: TrailWalkers during their employment cannot drink alcohol, smoke tobacco, or, awkwardly enough, have sexual relations. We are closer to monks than shrinks. Apart from a few ninja moves ANASAZI gave me in case of revolt (yes, TrailWalkers have been tied to trees before), our skills aspire to be nothing fancy.

My job description is basically to be loving, see the good in others, and be ready to help, which sounds more like a Girl Scout than a professional, and more demanding than a set of skills, especially if you were kicked out of Girl Scouts, as I was. A TrailWalker's skill is not specialized knowledge but acting in the face of not knowing. Responding thoughtfully and intuitively, physically and emotionally. I am woefully under-qualified, like everyone else. Thank god for group intelligence. Wilderness is in the business of utilizing inadequacy: through ours and the land's shortcomings, ANASAZI realizes its mission of having people learn to live on the land *with others*. We all lack too much to not be together.

ANASAZI takes pride in its emphasis on day-to-day desert living. No contrived consequences, it says, no psychological games. Dirt is dirt is dirt. In the desert, team-building and self-reflective challenges are built-in. Yet, how did the the kids end up in the wilderness in the first place? Artifice. Lying parents. Mine told me we were taking a road trip to visit my grandma. Ha! A father recently told his son they were taking a ride in a hot-air balloon. ("So, let me get this straight: is there a balloon?" he asked, dizzyingly, a week out in the desert.) Contrivance and scheming are often the only way to get kids to the wilderness, and once there, we live a charmed survival existence: everyone is going to make it. We are not surviving, we are playing survival. And it is this subtle entanglement of artifice and nature that is, I think, so productive. Wilderness therapy is not bare-boned reality, nor cause and effect at its purest. It is somewhere between performance and real-life, a performance for real-life: wandering in the wilderness for 40 days is, and long has been, role-playing.

+

We improvise and we impersonate. We imitate Indians. Survivalists. Hippies. Sages. We dance and howl under the moon, hold fire ceremonies, build hothouses out of willow, and can't resist chanting in them as the heat drips off our ochre-painted faces. We make moccasins and leather bags, use tools modeled after the ancients and sew with synthetic sinew. We use an invented group-speak, chock-full of romantic and tribal echoes. When I got home from ANASAZI as a teenager, I stopped shaving my legs or wearing a bra or using a bed. It was a performance of sorts. I was imitating what I had seen in my TrailWalkers, and I was acting out what I felt in myself—evolution—mighty and intangibly hairy. Yet the performance was one towards authenticity. Authenticity, that tertiary animal—it takes in others who have taken in others, mashes and mixes, incorporates part, and lets the rest pass through.

Our desert performance brings to mind Rumi's words: "Appear as you are, be as you appear." The sequence is confounding. There is no linear cause and effect, rather, the two clauses modify each other. The action is where the imperatives meet. *Appear as you are, be as you appear.* You can see the circle of seeming and becoming: as if is part of as is.

Fantasy is not always fooling yourself. It may amount to becoming yourself. As spontaneous and free as being who-you-are is, it is nothing if not proactive and retroactive. Besides, performance is a form of survival. It takes the edge off reality, which is quite sharp in the desert. "Acting like" creates a distance from ourselves that expands our possibilities. For instance, thinking like a stone can soften your steps, as *The Seven Paths of the ANASAZI Way* suggests:

I say this in all seriousness.
Don't be offended at the stone that turns beneath
your feet. After all, the stone isn't offended at you
even though you were the one who turned it.

That a stone could take offense at us is laughable, but then, maybe so is our anger when we trip over it. Impersonation opens us to the possibility of the impersonal, which is a particular interpretation and not the lack of one. An impersonal lens shows that you happen to the world as much as it happens to you—so don't take head bumping so personally. We're all playing here.

+

Even the plants are acting as if. They call it growing "adventitious roots." These roots are root impersonators, and true eccentrics in the plant world. The desert is drowning in them. Almost 200 species of cacti have exclusively adventitious roots, which grow not from other roots, but from stem or leaf tissue, making them sprout in unusual but fruitful places. They are versatile role-players, and often inspired by stress. If you're of an adventitious mind, stress lets the play begin. "If 'existence' is responded to as if it were less than totally in earnest," wrote Lionel Trilling, "spirit is the less bound by it. It can then without sadness accept existence, and without resentment transact such business with it as is necessary." Necessity is necessarily playful.

+

On top of the mountain, Rebecca chucks her pack into a crevice. It's 120 degrees out. *That there, that's not me.* Gabe and I are squatted on stones that could cook our asses sunny-side up. Our sunny sides are getting smoked, and our associations a bit scrambled. Scramble is a funny word, I say it over and over, as we fry on the rock with empty canteens. Can can can you do the can't can't can you... we haven't moved from this spot in a couple hours. *In a little while, I'll be gone, the moment's already passed, yeah it's gone.* We are in a rocky wash with no brush. Rebecca does not care to move towards shade or water. She does not care that without her pack she will have no food, no clothes, and no blanket tonight when it's cold.

Gabe is trying to use reason.

"How will you eat?"

"I'll go into the Boys Band and take all their food."

"How will you find them?"

"I'll howl till they get scared and cry and I hear where they are."

"How will you stay warm?"

"I'll go into the Boys Band and rape them and steal their blankets."

"Your plan is to rape the boys for warmth?"

I'd laugh if my throat weren't dried up. After Rebecca elucidates her plan to kill us all with the knife she's been too lazy to sharpen, we fall back into slumped staring. Jen and Marian are up ahead a ways, sharing some scrappy shade. I keep on with the song in my head. Emergency Radiohead for defibrillating detachment. *I'm not here, I'm not here, this isn't happening.*

+

The question I always hear is, "Does it work?," or its variant, "Does ANASAZI fix them?"—which sounds to me like a teen neutering, which meaning maybe isn't so far off: Do the kids permanently stop doing what they shouldn't? What is inconvenient to the parents? Do they stay sober? Do they quit cutting class? Are they nice to their mother? Do they stop hanging around those friends? According to these measurements, I was worse off after ANASAZI than before. Yet I consider myself a success story.

Often I'll tell kids that I was a YoungWalker like them. I'll also tell them that I came back four years later as a SinaguaWalker, that is, as a legal adult. What I never tell them is that, my second time in the program, I ran. And, contrary to the hopeless statistic I tell each group, I escaped ANASAZI. Why would I, who so loves the desert, run from it? Out of respect. The program does not modify behavior; it invites a way of being. That invitation, once internalized, never leaves. What more could the desert say to me? It was on me to choose to use or not use what had been given me. I ran, because I did not want to piss on sacred ground.

The wilderness does not make you change, but it does make you choose. Changes change, but choice is always there. This is why ANASAZI works even when it fails to fix.

Ok, but *how* does it work, parents insist. How does being outdoors heal people on the inside? The YoungWalkers share their doubts. They ask good questions: How is hiking around all day going to help me with my problems? Maddeningly and mysteriously the only answer to that is to keep hiking. I can't say why pushing through brush or trudging dry creek bed, one minute ducking, then leaping, scaling red ledges, edging along and behind and over and at times, in flushes of hot realization, in complete circles, help a person to think more clearly of herself, others, and the world. I have to suspect that mystery is part of the efficacy. Daily doses of the incalculable are good for growing humans.

+

Flora and fauna come to resemble each other in the desert. Extreme constraints breed creative redundancies. Solitary bees and desert flowers have both adapted to live much of the time underground. They speak the same language. As soon as the warm rains hit, the bees and seeds erupt from their earthen dens. Following the beat, they pick up their natural conversation as if no time had passed at all. There had been much time, in fact, much solitude and invisibility. Absence organizes a sticky liquid flying buzzing blooming attuned to the hearty world around it.

Desert rain does not fall on deaf ears. Believe it: bees and toads and rodents and fleshy seeds listen in holes underground.

+

The Chinese sages believed the bland to be healthy for mind and body. Blandness is the celery of the aesthetic diet—it gives us a workout with its slightness. We find ourselves crunching hard on air, burning off more than we're taking in. Understimulation, say the bland gurus, exercises the senses. Intensity leaves us with nothing to want, but boredom, boredom lingers. Intensively. What to do. You'll just have to occupy your self.

+

O the vapor of blandness! how it opens the spiritual sinuses.

Blandness, the interminable Mormon virtue. There is an oft-told story in Mormon circles that illustrates its high place in spiritual matters. Former President of the Church, Spencer W. Kimball, was once asked, "What do you do if you find yourself caught in a boring sacrament meeting?" The spiritual giant thought for a moment, then said, "I don't know; I've never been in one." Mormons know this to be a mightily ironic response because no one knows better than Mormons how boring they can be. The implication is that President Kimball was not simply hearing what there was to hear but generating something more. He who has ears to hear, let him hear something better than is said. Learning by the Spirit, as Mormons call it, means experiencing what is not present. It's a promise that no blah-blah is endured in vain, for "he shall mount up in the imagination of his thoughts as upon eagles' wings." When one is tempted to write off longsome tiresome ho-hum tedium, she is to contemplate filling in the blank.

What's in a Mormon Church, Temple, Desert, Get-together? Jazzed absence. Blandness takes the spike out of the punch and puts it in your brain.

+

The sun's down, but—high praises—so are we. Off the freaking mountain at last. Those of us who did not chuck our pack in a hole and leave it to rot, drop our stuff under our scraggly canopy of juniper. Jen and Marian waste no time in getting out fire sets and food. They down a handful of almonds and brown sugar lumps before setting to work on the fire. Rebecca eyes Jen's opened sugar bag.

I'm too worn out to care about food. Gabe hasn't moved or spoken since we put down our packs. He sits hunched on the ground like a comatose toad. No sooner do we exhale, Wind comes upon us.

WindWalker is an exalted TrailWalker, a lone ranger. He or she roams free of any Band in order to help all Bands. Sometimes this is life-saving. Other times, Wind blowing through your camp can be totally deflating. Some Winds police as much as they doctor. Wind pops in, fresh and perky from a lone cowboy camp, energetically wins over our group, making us look like sticks in the mud. Then tells us what we can do better. At those times, Wind is the grandparent of the Trail, rolling in, spoiling our kids, lending unasked advice, then leaving us to deal.

Our Wind is not the ranger you'd expect. He wears trousers and a sweater vest. He is small and impeccably cheery. His boyish

look belies his experience, as does his use of obscure, old-fashioned
swears, like "gosh-all-Potomac!" or "blistering barnacles!" Once,
his first week out on the Trail, in freezing January, his pack got
swept down the Verde River as he and the group struggled to
cross. Some camper found it eventually and turned it over to the
park rangers. From its clothing content, they thought some poor
80-year-old man had washed down the river. Wind was delighted
to get his green sweater vest back.

"Howdydoo! Permission to enter camp?" Wind enters our
circle and shows the kids his new papoose, gorgeously beaded and
fringed. He sings a merry song before asking to powwow with the
TrailWalkers. Me and James try to look alive as we follow him off
a ways.

Wind tells us what we already know and can't imagine.

"You have to hike back up and get that pack. And Rebecca
has to choose to do it with you."

The first part sounds unpleasant, the second unfathomable,
and the two, at any rate, are at odds. Leaving the pack there isn't
an option, yet we must give Rebecca the option. ANASAZI's
emphasis on agency really ties our hands back. James and I laugh
but Wind doesn't. He doesn't know Rebecca. No substance on
earth could induce that girl to turn around and hike back up that
mountain.

I have to eat my words. Wind and Rebecca have a private
Sitting for an hour, and when they rejoin the group, Rebecca tells
us she is ready to go. James and I are shocked, chastised. Why
didn't we have more faith in her "seed of greatness"? Wind has
out-zenned us.

Halfway up the mountain Rebecca furtively takes a little
baggie out of her pocket. A full Ziplock of glistening blue Tang.
No one in our group could have such a stash. *Genius*. ANASAZI
has its Ideals, but thank god even the exalted ones condescend to
bribery.

+

As iconic as the American desert has become—all three-armed cactus and cow skull and moon-puckered coyote—the desert is the iconoclast of ecology. The very definition of desert is debated. Dry, hot, salty and barren. A desert may be all or none of these things. The Arctic has been called a "polar desert," and the open sea—there are not many places wetter—"oceanic desert." The root of "desert" means "forsaken" or "abandoned." And this seems to be our measure of it: desert is a place that is lacking. A place apparently empty, full of less obvious life.

Get a bunch of geographers in a room and they'll mostly agree that deserts are defined by their aridity. However, ask how arid a region must be or how best to measure this aridity, and some rocks might fly. It is better, suggest some, to think of arid regions as a continuum of environments, measured in degrees rather than absolutes. The desert likely has no boundary.

It seems we are constantly crossing into other worlds as we hike: a morning of flat cracked earth, noon on a scruffy mountain, midday in a ponderosa forest carpeted with pine needles, and a canyon-deep evening along a rushing stream.

The desert's continuum also runs vertical. Each landscape has another landscape underneath and waiting to pop up. I remember a day a few summers ago, I was in Girls Band, and we were trudging up the spine of a bone-dry creek bed. Everything was rock and gray. Almost all at once the air turned incredibly heavy as low clouds smothered the sky. We were rounding a mountain of black-charcoaled trees when the rain dumped. It pooled improbably, and greens seeped out of nowhere. The landscape was becoming fluid like a dream. What I'll never forget: moon-white flowers unfurling like bat wings. They were everywhere, spooking at dark raindrops. They beamed pale against the burned-up trees, the sky's boiling gray. There was something mammal-like about them that repulsed and enthralled. I don't remember them having any purple, but I always think *purplish-shade* when I remember. Perhaps because it sounds vaguely poisonous. To this day I don't know what these flowers are, and honestly, I'm not interested. They remain the plant of my dreams.

+

Brigham Young told his desert people in 1852: "Progress and improve upon and make beautiful everything around you. Cultivate the earth and cultivate your minds.... make gardens, orchards and vineyards, and render the earth so pleasant that when you look upon your labors you may do so with pleasure, and that the angels may delight to come and visit your beautiful locations." And so the desert became the ground of the Mormon imagination.

A non-Mormon visitor to Salt Lake City commented that Young seemed to fuse spiritual enlightenment and landscape building, preaching "exaltation in heaven" one Sunday, and the next, "how to irrigate and drain land, harvest crops, set out trees, beautify their grounds...." Perceiving the potential of the desert became itself a religious practice.

Mormons were trained, spiritually and practically, to colonize wastelands. The Church sent out hundreds of groups of converts to establish Mormon oases across the wilderness: Eastern Utah, Nevada, Idaho, Arizona. My ancestors, converts come to Salt Lake from Scandinavia, were told to uproot once again and blaze their way to the dry, flat, empty heart of Arizona. They did, and they built, and they spread, leaving only briefly, once plural wives were outlawed in the U.S., for the Mexican side of nowhere, and when those houses got razed by revolutionaries and sunk back into the sun-baked mud, they returned to Arizona as if it were home all along.

Even today, any good Mormon will move in a heartbeat when asked to do so by the Church. Home, by these lights, is not where you live, but where you're led. This is an old story of the wilderness.

+

Desert as a moral and social guide is not a breakthrough of modern psychology, new coat of "wilderness therapy" notwithstanding. Jesus and Muhammad spent significant time in deserts, and Moses, poor Moses, couldn't lead his people any other way.

The story of Abraham begins without preamble: Get lost. *Go forth from your native land, from your birthplace, and from your father's house to the land that I will show you.* Come undone in the desert. Leave everything you were about to be for nothing you could say with any certainty. Become other, which is finally you.

Lekh lekha—literally, "Go to yourself."

The Book of Mormon starts with a family commanded to leave iniquitous Jerusalem and enter the barren desert. They must uproot, reorient, begin again. The people carrying this book split from American society to set up their own State in the wilderness.

Intrinsic to desert is testing ground. It is where humans go to either escape from or conceal extreme corruption. The story across time/space: Man leaves behind the comfort and spoils of society and turns toward an indefinite integrity. He takes to the blank of the desert to re-imagine what man is about. He writes. The words sink into dust. We who are made of dust take to translating them.

+

When I first started TrailWalking for ANASAZI, I wanted to be put with the boys. They're stronger, I concluded, lazily. They'll be faster hikers, better fire-makers. Gradually I learned my mistake. Ask any TrailWalker who has been there and back with both groups, and they'll tell you the same thing: The girls have the most endurance. This is the truth of my women ancestors crossing the desert with their homes tied up in wagons, children on their hips, the husband ahead or behind. I didn't come to their stories until later. Women to me are the long-run surprise.

One of the aims of the Mormon colonizing expeditions of the 1870s was to establish peaceful relationships with the Indians. This meant traveling through Navajo territory—tough, red land. White heat. Black winds. In our family history journals from this expedition I found the story of one of my foremothers giving birth on the rocky backbone between the Colorado and San Juan Rivers. When the family reached a plateau, a blizzard was raging, and exposed to the wild winds and snows, the woman went into labor. The husband tried to pitch a tent as she pushed. As the baby emerged, a hard slapping wind came and blew the tent upward. The woman reached up and held the pole down with one hand, the baby, now, in the other.

The desert is full of holy tents full of holy men and holy smoke of manly meats for the man-god behind the curtain. But when I hear *the Lord dwelt in a tent*, all I see inside is my foremother using her body as a stake as she pushes out human life.

+

Give any slob a compass and a machete and they'll look all business. The desert is maybe the only place where the more rugged you look, the more professional you seem. With my pink tentacles of greasy hair, rainbow button-up shirt complete with duck tape patches, and wool pants with a wide smile of stitches across the ass—I look masterful.

The truth is, I'm bad with maps. The problem is deeper than that: I am spatially handicapped. I always have been. I exist in a geographical blackout. It does not matter how long I stare, I cannot match a squiggle on the page to a ridge on the land to save my life, which is the point. I am a wilderness guide after all. What complicates matters even more is that I cannot locate the direction of sound. I have only one ear that hears. ANASAZI uses a hooting system— a very distinct yawp—to communicate and navigate within and between Bands. This can prove crucial if, say, the group gets split up for whatever reason and you must find one another in a vast and hairy landscape. You don't want to go up the wrong mountain. Which is exactly what I have done. It's shameful. Is that a hoot? Watch my good ear spin in circles to catch it. Like a dog chasing its nub of tail.

So how have I gotten this far? Moderate wits, fat luck, and, unfortunately for my group, endless trial and error. Fortunately for me, they don't know that. Circles in a barren place are hard to recognize. The desert is discreet.

I have taken our group to the wrong cow tank, and it is dry, and we are out of water, like we have been since yesterday. Everyone is in bad shape. Barely speak. Wolf mouth, shut, keep moisture in. Brain cooks, thoughts waft in small o smoke rings. W a t e r e s c a p e. We've stepped into delusional. We've dropped our packs on the cracked mudbank and are resting our aching backs of wasted wet against them. No one says anything. Rebecca picks up a rock and scratches big letters into the dry skin of her arm: S-E-X. Someone must have another idea.

+

Another ancestress of mine gave birth in a tent in the desert. She was a second wife. Part of an outlawed but covenant union. There is no heavenly hurt quite like a commanded threesome. Following the exodus from Mexico, the fugitive family stopped long enough for her to give birth to a son in a government tent. There, a few days later, she was abandoned by her husband, his other wife and their family, and left with a young daughter, a newborn, and a desert. She and her children never saw her husband again. She chose to make that desert and solitude her home, refusing to move, refusing to remarry, calling it her life.

Stories repeat in the desert. Wives turn each other out, houses split, lines continue. Hagar weeps, God sees, wells appear, histories proliferate. And descendants plumb the depths.

It wasn't until my grandma was an adult with her own family that she discovered her mother had been part of a polygamous household. The second wife had never been spoken of. As the secret cracked, bit by bit, correspondences opened between the families. It was found that the two wives, in their old age—husband long dead—had written letters. "As I look back over the years I think of those days we lived together. We were so closely associated and had trials and many things came up which could have been avoided if only we had been more patient and kind.... Eva dear, with all my heart and in deep humility I ask you to forgive me, that we may live in unity, love and happiness in the hereafter." Sarah and Hagar never met again. But in the 1940s and 50s they sent postcards across the desert between them.

In the desert, stories repeat until they change. Echoes bring the rockslide.

+

Blandness has no stake in any one thing.

Revelation and epiphany only cramp the bland's style. Conclusions forgo it. Much preferred is the logic inherent in change itself. In the landscape of blandness, extremes express not themselves but each other: one state passing into another. States waving their own lack of allegiance.

The bland carries the world on the shrug of its shoulders. It lets itself be led from one extreme to another, with as little intervention as possible.

+

There should be water right—here. A sad empty bed, the color of old oyster meat, stares up at us from where the map showed a solid blue circle. This is not good, this is not good. This is not a mantra Gabe and I say out loud.

"Ok guys, sit tight, I'm just gonna take the radio and go up on that hill to check in, alright?" But my voice quakes.

Gabe and I lock eyes for a second. He's as much at a loss as I am. Even if he knew better, it is not the ANASAZI way to take the maps out of somebody's hands, no matter how tenuous their grip. Efficiency is not our meat.

I know this. I know it's about "experience," but I don't sense the great possibilities of failure when failure is sucking our bodies and brains dry. I'm charging too fast up the rocky cliff in my Chacos, radio in one hand, the other pumping and grasping at boulders, shredding my fingertips, the rocks and I mixing our grits. There's no reason to kill myself, but it feels good. I feel guilty and useless. As if these girls weren't struggling enough as it is. I can't even get them to freaking water and the sun will go down and they'll be miserable and angry and probably write blistering letters home and then their parents will be on the defensive and a whole new spat of tit-for-tat will begin and no one's hearts will heal or grades improve and the girls will drop out of high school with vague talk of a GED and deliver pizzas to the door of a life they almost had but lost to dehydration.

I am having my TrailWalker meltdown moment. Radios are for checking in, but we also use them as a device for taking off to fall apart in private. Long check-ins are understood. I am where the hill levels out, lying on my back, sharp stones digging between my ribs, and I am crying like a dehydrated drama queen with low blood sugar. When I turn my face there's a cow staring at me. There are three or four up on this mound, probably looking for the same tank we were.

ANASAZI 101: *You are not the healer.* Agree as you might, there is always some sneaky part of you that tries anyway. This part dooms itself to an illusion: lack as shortcoming. Which is a shortage of imagination: failure as failure.

+

Wilderness doesn't allow for guides, only seekers. No person—whatever their age or expertise—is beyond growing pains. Everyone is learning their limits, and tripping past them.

A mom came out for Family Camp—the two-day reunion on the Trail of child and parents—and pulled a ballistic kid stunt: she ran away. The desert drove her nuts. She tried to book it for a road, any goddamn road. A TrailWalker recently hopped in the emergency vehicle before the week's end and refused to get out. Two months from now, dear Gabe, according to his own Walking, will have an epic freakout, to be named The Vanishing, and will not return for six months.

Self-discovery is not a transcendent journey. It's a private tantrum in a public place where you are both child and parent. The desert is space to let it all play out. *With as little intervention as possible.* Go on and kick and scream and cuss and throw that stupid pack down a hole and spit on it like you mean it. The desert won't flinch. It only makes picking it back up unavoidable.

+

Sikong Tu, an illustrious poet of blandness, sang of a sweet spot somewhere between sterile and volatile. He wrote a cycle of poems to show what he called the twenty-four poetic modes. These poems have names like Harmony-Blandness, Force-Incipiency, Shimmer-Beauty, and the especially splendid Limpid-Sublime. Blandness plays between these poles. Unfixed, its balance can only be lost and regained, lost and regained, the hyphen a teeter-totter of attraction. Hyphens do interesting work. The meaning of each title exists not in the words but the relationship between them. With a single dash, content gets underwritten by chemistry.

Chemistry, that limpid-sublime stuff of live-wire I-thou encounter constantly threatened with obliteration. Martin Buber, whose *I And Thou* underlies much of ANASAZI philosophy, invented an opaque-lucid language to show, like Sikong Tu's binomials, that our most basic units are relations. ANASAZI, in the hyphenate spirit of I-thou, has created its own language by pairing Buber and Navajo ideas. What Buber calls an "I-thou relation," ANASAZI talks about as a Heart-at-peace. What Buber calls "return," ANASAZI calls a New Beginning. Like the balance of blandness, a Heart-at-peace is transitory. It will lapse into seeing people as objects and objects as more than people. I once heard someone ask Ezekiel how it is then that you hold on to a Heart-at-peace. He said, "you don't." You keep getting one.

+

It's midday, the day after we should be at Final D, and we break at a creek: sit our bums down in the sweet cool mud, soak our blistered feet, and Gabe and I know our destination is just around the canyon's corner. A mile and a half or so. So doable, so done. We did it. Damn we're good.

We dry off some on the rocks then wriggle back into our packs and boots, ready. Hallelujah. The end is really here, when Rebecca up and chooses a different ending.

"I'm not moving."

Girl down.

No one is sure how to take this. Downright senseless. Not that Rebecca has been a paragon of sense, but this move is so extravagantly backwards that I don't even know how to bribe her. Rebecca wants to be at Final D, where she knows that she a) won't have to hike for a few days, b) gets letters and FOOD and clean underwear, and c) can slap her yells off canyon walls like a little monkey in heat for all the boys camped at Final D to hear. She knows all this is a very short hike away. She knows she doesn't like hiking in the dark, and she knows we need to leave now for that not to happen.

And yet, "I'm not moving." Whether or not she knows what she means by it, she means it. We are not going anywhere.

After the first hour passes, Jen and Marian, patient, coaxing, even babying, move to dramatic, pleading, tearful, and after the second and third hour, threatening, sobbing, yelling, now sulking under the hot sun apart from Rebecca staked out under the one shade tree.

This is what ANASAZI calls a Heart-at-war. Gabe and I move and moderate between the girls. I am calm and patient with Rebecca, but it's no use because I am these things out of self-interest. The Heart-at-war that smiles is just as useless as the one that kicks and screams. So I shut my mouth and close my eyes. Put myself in her place. Which is to say, I fumble around a 13-year-old girl's brain until a crack opens and some grace slips in, and being Rebecca becomes real. My heart hurts and I can see her. And I see peace has to come from the other two girls.

Who are these girls? I go to where they are sunk down and sullen on the dirt. We talk about a Heart-at-peace and what it means. I leave to fill my canteens. When I walk back Rebecca has her pack on and Jen and Marian are helping her tighten the straps using bandanas. I blink hard. These are astonishing humans. What on earth did the two girls say? How did Rebecca respond? Doesn't matter. I feel it. The under-stated power I come back to the desert for.

+

When I returned home from ANASAZI as a girl, almost a woman, I remember seeing the desert as the meridian of my life. Me, my world, my relationships, divided into life before and after the wilderness. This would prove to be untrue. I would run from and return to the desert more times and in more ways than fit on two sides of a map. The meridian curved. Because, for starters, the desert is a cycle.

Lattice Through Which I Glimpsed Something There

```
?????!      ??????!      ??????!      ??????!      ??????!      ?????
???? !!!!!!    ???? !!!!!!    ???? !!!!!!    ???? !!!!!!    ???? !!!!!!    ????
??? !!!!!!!!!!   ??? !!!!!!!!!!   ??? !!!!!!!!!!   ??? !!!!!!!!!!   ??? !!!!!!!!!!   ???
? !!!!!!!!!!!!!   ? !!!!!!!!!!!!!   ? !!!!!!!!!!!!!   ? !!!!!!!!!!!!!   ? !!!!!!!!!!!!!   ?
!!!!!!!!!!!!!!!   ? !!!!!!!!!!!!!!   ? !!!!!!!!!!!!!!   ? !!!!!!!!!!!!!!   ? !!!!!!!!!!!!!!   ?
!!!!!!!!!!!! ???   !!!!!!!!!!!! ???   !!!!!!!!!!!! ???   !!!!!!!!!!!! ???   !!!!!!!!!!!! ???
!!!!!!!!!!??????   !!!!!!!!!!??????   !!!!!!!!!!??????   !!!!!!!!!!??????   !!!!!!!!!!??????
!!!!!!??????   !!!!!!??????   !!!!!!??????   !!!!!!??????   !!!!!!??????
!???????   !???????   !???????   !???????   !???????
!    ??????!      ??????!      ??????!      ??????!      ??????!
!!!!    ???? !!!!!!    ???? !!!!!!    ???? !!!!!!    ???? !!!!!!    ???? !!!!!!
!!!!!    ??? !!!!!!!!!!   ??? !!!!!!!!!!   ??? !!!!!!!!!!   ??? !!!!!!!!!!   ??? !!!!!!!!!!
!!!!!!!   ? !!!!!!!!!!!!!   ? !!!!!!!!!!!!!   ? !!!!!!!!!!!!!   ? !!!!!!!!!!!!!   ?
!!!!!!!!!   ? !!!!!!!!!!!!!!   ? !!!!!!!!!!!!!!   ? !!!!!!!!!!!!!!   ? !!!!!!!!!!!!!!   ?
!!!!!!!! ???   !!!!!!!!!!!! ???   !!!!!!!!!!!! ???   !!!!!!!!!!!! ???   !!!!!!!!!!!! ???   !!!!!!!!!!!!
!!!!!!??????   !!!!!!!!!!??????   !!!!!!!!!!??????   !!!!!!!!!!??????   !!!!!!!!!!??????   !!!!!!!!!!?
!!!!??????   !!!!!!??????   !!!!!!??????   !!!!!!??????   !!!!!!??????   !!!!!!??
!???????   !???????   !???????   !???????   !???????   !???
??????!      ??????!      ??????!      ??????!      ??????!      ???
???? !!!!!!    ???? !!!!!!    ???? !!!!!!    ???? !!!!!!    ???? !!!!!!    ???
??? !!!!!!!!!!   ??? !!!!!!!!!!   ??? !!!!!!!!!!   ??? !!!!!!!!!!   ??? !!!!!!!!!!   ???
? !!!!!!!!!!!!!   ? !!!!!!!!!!!!!   ? !!!!!!!!!!!!!   ? !!!!!!!!!!!!!   ? !!!!!!!!!!!!!   ?
? !!!!!!!!!!!!!!   ? !!!!!!!!!!!!!!   ? !!!!!!!!!!!!!!   ? !!!!!!!!!!!!!!   ? !!!!!!!!!!!!!!   ?
!!!!!!!!!!!! ???   !!!!!!!!!!!! ???   !!!!!!!!!!!! ???   !!!!!!!!!!!! ???   !!!!!!!!!!!! ???
!!!!!!!!!!??????   !!!!!!!!!!??????   !!!!!!!!!!??????   !!!!!!!!!!??????   !!!!!!!!!!??????
!!!!!!??????   !!!!!!??????   !!!!!!??????   !!!!!!??????   !!!!!!??????
!???????   !???????   !???????   !???????   !???????
!    ??????!      ??????!      ??????!      ??????!      ??????!
!!!!    ???? !!!!!!    ???? !!!!!!    ???? !!!!!!    ???? !!!!!!    ???? !!!!!!
!!!!!    ??? !!!!!!!!!!   ??? !!!!!!!!!!   ??? !!!!!!!!!!   ??? !!!!!!!!!!   ??? !!!!!!!!!!
!!!!!!!   ? !!!!!!!!!!!!!   ? !!!!!!!!!!!!!   ? !!!!!!!!!!!!!   ? !!!!!!!!!!!!!   ? !!!!!!!!!!!!!
!!!!!!!!!   ? !!!!!!!!!!!!!!   ? !!!!!!!!!!!!!!   ? !!!!!!!!!!!!!!   ? !!!!!!!!!!!!!!   ? !!!!!!!!!!!!!!
!!!!!!!! ???   !!!!!!!!!!!! ???   !!!!!!!!!!!! ???   !!!!!!!!!!!! ???   !!!!!!!!!!!! ???   !!!!!!!!!!!!
!!!!!!??????   !!!!!!!!!!??????   !!!!!!!!!!??????   !!!!!!!!!!??????   !!!!!!!!!!??????   !!!!!!!!!!
!!!!??????   !!!!!!??????   !!!!!!??????   !!!!!!??????   !!!!!!??????   !!!!!!?
!???????   !???????   !???????   !???????   !???????   !??
```

Plant Inter/eruption

It's not odd but it is somewhat rare for kids who were abducted by ANASAZI to come back later in life as guides. When I came of TrailWalker age, I did not race back to the desert, gourd canteen in hand and bright and bushy bandana-ed. I came back on my face, years later, conscripted by what escapes me.

It was one of those seasons when a Beatles lyric diabolically inverts and repeats like a mantra in your brain. In my case, late spring, when the snow was just starting to melt off the mountains in Salt Lake City, it was no longer about all the lonely people, where do they all come from, but, dammit, where do they all *go to*? Lately I had become aware of a sort of ghostly double-vision— or, rather, an eerie conviction that I *should* be seeing double. I would hike up a frost-slick hill overlooking the white-domed Capitol building and dark vein of creek pumping through the park below. I would splay out on the wet grass and fling off my clunky skid-proof shoes, damp socks, loosen my pastel Olive Garden tie, and take yogic breaths like a dog or the ocean, and then the uncanny expectation would seize me. Shouldn't I look over and see someone, like myself, sprawled on the grass, sweaty-footed, possibly tacky neck-tied, and consciously breathing the selfsame air? Or, when I stalked the sidewalks at night, I felt pangs, like footfalls, the footfalls that should've been echoing my own, from the other side of the street. Then there was the flitter in my chest of the pages that should've been turning of the same book I was reading, from the bench next to mine, in the unmowed Pioneer Memorial garden off my road. But there was no one sitting or striding or reading parallel to myself.

I don't think the feeling that there ought to be was one of romantic fantasy or mere narcissism. It was more like a kinetic sense of the senselessness of being only one body. I was sure others—whole streets, cities, planets of them—were experiencing the same impossible isolation I was, so why weren't we all running into each other—nay, falling over each other—on the lonely road? It seemed more spooky to *not* have a clone. A strange sensation: life is an amputee. And symmetry is the phantom limb. And something, something in all this is the walrus. All the lonely people, where do they all go to?

Why does anybody get lonely? Not for lack of people. Holy shit, so many people. I had an old friend in Salt Lake. We had lived and worked together for a time in Prague. I had come home after two years working abroad, in between places and phases, and she offered me her sofa. 2011 in Salt Lake City saw the highest precipitation levels recorded since 1870; over 3,000 people stripped to their bras, panties, and boxer shorts jogging through the streets in what organizers called the "Undie Run," protesting the uptight laws of Utah; the countdown for America's first shopping center with (1.5 billion dollar) retractable glass roofs, parallel to the Mormon Temple; The Decemberists in a free, packed and steamy concert at Pioneer Park; and during their opening song, the death of our dear friend in a freak mountain-biking accident on a trail outside the city.

But before any of that, my first night in Salt Lake, I got lost. Just as soon as I panicked I walked over a compass, inlaid in gold in the sidewalk. I embraced it as a sign. A sealing of my choice to come to Salt Lake and get my bearings. And in the end I would, but of course no where near the way I thought.

I was awed by my friend's apartment when I first walked in. It was so—grown-uppity. The walls were filled with paintings that matched the colors of the rug that matched the pots of houseplants that matched the kitchen seat cushions that were surrounded by clean counters with glass jars full of nuts and rice and noodles, not to eat, just to look at. The very books on her shelf appeared part of the color scheme. Weren't we the same age? I didn't have a pillow to my name, and here she was with a color-coordinated cornucopia of bed cushions so gigantic that crawling under the covers required something like the dismantling of a lego castle. My friend handed me a faux Indian pillow bejeweled with shiny bits and funky textures, which, while slouching towards the couch, I realized played off the turquoise of the curtains, and I knew my rootless ass was out of its league. She would teach me how to be a real person.

Being a person is learned, and learning takes time, and time she and I didn't have much of—we both had jobs, and depression, which exists in a timezone all its own—and to each other we were barely people.

We both had been Mormon missionaries in Albania. That is how we met. So that is who we had to be to each other. But that is not who we were. If you were tall as god and bothered to look down, you would have seen two girls, separated by a wall, one stuck on a couch and one sunk on a bed, and both nursing a drink, and each hiding it from the other when the other passed through the doorway between them, each girl believing she was the odd Mormon out.

It wasn't long before the aesthetic of the apartment flattened from impressive to oppressive. There was a self-enclosing order—baring down from every perfectly executed wall—that exhausted me. I ached for a fixed home, but hated the fixedness of a deliberate house. I started spending long hours outside, whole days, some nights. My friend was spending her nights somewhere else, too. I stopped sleeping. The world looked off-kilter and it kept me reeling. At times, objects appeared to have come unglued from their backdrops and hung around me like discrete, disconnected units, myself a discrete disconnected unit, each thing made in the image of nothing at all. It was clear my brain needed a reality facelift. For a week I called the number of a so-called Zen Buddhist office eight blocks over, and the phone would ring and ring and ring. I would trudge down there, knock on the door, smoosh my face to the glass. Window blinds down, locked up, lights off. All I wanted to know, people, was what is what!

Of course I also wanted people. Or, to say it from my organs, where I felt it — to have a people. Though I was not born or raised in Utah—countries far from it—as a Mormon it was my inherited home and, finding myself an adult without one, I thought I would lay claim to it. Reclaim old friends and rituals, and I hoped, old certainties.

Before setting out my Father had put his hands on my head and blessed me in the name of the Lord to find joy and comfort in reuniting with the body of the Saints, but failed to mention what that body looked like. Salt Lake is a split-brain body of right and left. Utah itself a reactive state: built on them and us and theirs and ours, Mormons become hyper-Mormon in the face of non-Mormons who become hyper not-Mormon right back in their face. Then there is the polarity within Utah Mormonism, as those who don't want to be pegged as Utah Mormons must go out of their way to turn it inside out, and so switch up the side-parts of their hair-do's and grow out mustaches (the maximum facial hair allowed at the private Mormon University) and act out a more self-conscious brand of Mormonism's innate nerdiness. You can see where this is going: Salt Lake is Hipster Zion. It is Brooklyn, with a Temple, and without, of course, black people. And it was the worst real estate in the universe for finding middle ground.

In the beginning I tried reaching out to some people, but then I stopped, because I didn't know which kind of a person I was.

The kinetic-clonetic sense that haunted my experience of Salt Lake came to a head a certain 3 a.m. on the vintage burgundy sofa. I had just woken up from a dream in which I was on the same sofa feeling exactly as I did awake on the sofa. It's bad when you can't even escape reality in your dreams. The difference was that the phone rang next to the dream-sofa. In my dream, I picked up. A voice said, *It's God on the other line and he says the World wants to talk to you.* I said, *Tell God I don't want to talk right now.* And that was it. Abruptly awake on the hard-fact sofa, I looked over to see no one else had just woken up from the same dream. This was too much to bear. As if to take the physical balance of the universe into my own hands, my arms shot straight up to the ceiling, fingers branched to unnatural lengths on each hand. They held until the blood drained down and the tingly numbness set in and my eyes were stuck shut with gummy wetness. Here was my challenge to the yawning negligence of the cosmos! I would wrestle symmetry to the earth with pitifulness! I would picket my arms up in the air until something would meet their reach with equal weight! I passed out waiting.

Ok, I suppose what I was really saying was, hug me.

The morning saw me with a clown face of bright fuschia and turquoise smeared down one side. The imprint of my friend's fancy pillow—clearly not to be washed with emotion. It seemed somehow false to scrub the absurdity off me, so I put on my shoes, as is, ran out the door. Arms stiff, but swinging, legs picking up, off at a crazed pace. Up the hill, down, along the black creek, into the canyon. My usual trail. I made it to my turn around point, about four miles up. But instead of heading back I found myself veering a sharp left, off the path, starting up a hill, winter-pickled grass brittle and crunching under my shoes. I mean that in its visceral sense: I *found* myself veering. My movements were discovered by me in the act of their happening. I was along for the ride.

Trail behind me, it started with a dew drop.

There was a leaf, which it magnified. Forgive me, I hardly know the names of plants. I simply smile recognition as they come. This one was low growing, a peach-fuzzy stalk with straight-edged leaves all around and tapering to its tip. The dew drop was cradled where leaf met stalk. It glinted the sun and shot me in the eye. I found myself dropped to knees to look into light. My heart beat prismatic, my finger tapped the leaf, the dew bounced its way down from blade to blade, never breaking, sparkling, a self-contained sunburst. Good god! I exhaled. That there could be something so lit up. On hands and knees I crawled to the next stalk—loaded with drops, me dropping them, them holding round, holding the sun, now caught in the play of the bounce of my hands. There was something I wanted. I stuck a fat dew drop with the tip of my tongue. Oh. It burst in my mouth like a taut grape. Crawling low, on to the next one, lips to leaf, again, again, slurping like a drunk bee. The drops fell, down the stalks, down my cheeks, all together. Oh. Smiling huge, laughing loud, pouring tears. Oh oh oh. Happiness is wild.

I think I'm full, when I turn and see the stone. Oh. On it

aqua and green splattered lichen, a hand-print of fractal fingers. Hand-printing: I was here. I'm here. A voice from ground level:

I've been waiting for you.

I buried my face into the hand. Or, I found myself curled up forehead to rock.

What someone else saw:

She left the trail. Ran straight up the hill. Next, she just hit the dirt. Looked like she was lickin' the ground brush. I heard laughter, real goofylike. Finally she just bangin' her head against a rock and makin' noise like a hurt animal. We didn't say nothin'. You get those kind up here.

The eye owes its existence to the light, said Goethe. Whoever or whatever you are, in you the light has produced an organ corresponding to itself. Eons before your first sight, organs sensitive to light saw to the earth with their whole body. Photosynthesizing plants have been around for hundreds of millions of years. You know the sensation of being watched. You know an eye when you feel one. Don't tell me the peachy weed plant off the trail couldn't have been eyeing me because it hasn't got one. It is one.

There's a way I've taken to explaining the root of all this to myself. That maddening sense of transbodily imbalance—of clonelessness, unwitnessedness—was not just some mad riot in my brain. My body was onto something. There should be living symmetry. For every thing that sees there should be a seer. For every thing that knows there should be a knower. For every thing should be a damn thing. I've gone in circles enough times to be suspicious of "lasting change." But, as it is, from the moment I slurped the droppy dew from leaf fuzz, the nervous tic of singleness went from my flesh.

God's on the line, and he says the World wants to talk to you.

What someone else sees:

Now you always make eye contact with trees.

Now, mornings, you move through tree-lined streets like a crowd-surfer. You buoy your body passing branch to branch. Brush leaves, press trunks, palm moss, all moving you along. How you walk is tree to tree to tree. Once a fellow passerby asked if you were OCD. Another, if you were the Gardner.

You learned this art as a kid. Monkey bars: it's all up in the air, but either behind you or in front of you—there's a grip. Keep your eye on the branches and keep moving. Monkey bars tell the secret: eye contact, handhold, and the groove.

You take the route through the park twice a day. You're getting seen, felt in your hands.

Trees are eyes popped out of their sockets. All groundburst veins, iris and light flecks—dark trunk down the center a projectile pupil. These, trees, are eyes trans-fixed. Once you thought your eye was what an eye is. But, oh man, an eye has infinite looks.

You are making eyes at trees, holding that they see you. A new kind of blind faith.

As I ran back down the trail I was panting happiness. Wonder pumped through my limbs and I moved like a free animal. *The Earth has a voice.* I hadn't known, or maybe I did but forgot, and now that I remembered, I couldn't be sure of anything that I knew. Life was fundamentally different than when I set out that morning with a sad clown face—now sweated and dewed away. Life was a Yes.

Yes already, so I should stop trying so hard. So I should forget Zion. Forget the Zen hotline. Get back to the wilderness, back to wildness. Yes, join that peculiar sanity of a de-sanitized people—wilderness therapy guides—in the Arizona desert. Back there, where I'd been sent as a kid, a kid who wanted to die. That kid wasn't wrong in what she felt: life's complex, it's both layered and empty, and it's lonely, and truth is a desert showing signs of a lost sea. Time to go back, way out there, as a woman. For just a beat I felt a no, no, not the discomfort. Not the hunger, the heat, those headaches. Not all that again. But the Yes drowns them out. I quit my job waiting tables that night. Got out of town. And have stayed out. I don't know if God's on the line. But the World wants to talk to me, and the desert is empty enough to hear.

eye sees yes sees eye

```
e y e s e e y e s e e y e s s e y e e s e y e e s e y e
e e y e s e e y e s e e y e e y e e s e y e e s e y e e
s e e y e s e e y e s e e y y e e s e y e e s e y e e s
e s e e y e s e e y e s e e e e s e y e e s e y e e s e
y e s e e y e s e e y e s e e s e y e e s e y e e s e y
e y e s e e y e s e e y e s s e y e e s e y e e s e y e
y e s e e y e s e e y e s e e s e y e e s e y e e s e y
e s e e y e s e e y e s e e e e s e y e e s e y e e s e
s e e y e s e e y e s e e   e e s e y e e s e y e e s
e e y e s e e y e s e e         e e s e y e e s e y e e
e y e s e e y e s e e           e e s e y e e s e y e
e y e s e e y e s e e           e e s e y e e s e y e
e e y e s e e y e s e e         e e s e y e e s e y e e
s e e y e s e e y e s e e   e e s e y e e s e y e e s
e s e e y e s e e y e s e e e e s e y e e s e y e e s e
y e s e e y e s e e y e s e e s e y e e s e y e e s e y
e y e s e e y e s e e y e s s e y e e s e y e e s e y e
y e s e e y e s e e y e s e e s e y e e s e y e e s e y
e s e e y e s e e y e s e e e e s e y e e s e y e e s e
s e e y e s e e y e s e e y y e e s e y e e s e y e e s
e e y e s e e y e s e e y e e y e e s e y e e s e y e e
e y e s e e y e s e e y e s s e y e e s e y e e s e y e
```

²b r o o d

Leaving off the sound of the thing, which is in fact a low
lug of foghorn, a meaty throb of longing pitted in blank
space.And forgetting for a moment the physiology of it—
the lips loosely puckered with a cigarist's musculature,
and, yes, bluesily blowing a smoke-ring in life's face.
Let's not break up the phonemes, for I have an ex who, in
discussions without solutions, would occasionally rap the
closest hard surface—just once—with the boney head of
his knuckle in what I took to be a terse expression of *Welp
that's the way it is*—a shrug of a plunk, folk-punctuation
that hits like a knowing glance, and that's how the tail-end
d strikes me in my mouth. Besides, if you were to tell it,
you'd have to go to the start: speak the *br*—a bumble like
a half-hearted belch—trailing into the cyclical ache of *oo*,
to end a thump of tongue against the wall of your teeth—
duh. So now you've gone and done it: you've burbled
a sigh, you've mouthed the pout, you've pronounced a
dull thunk *that's just how it is*. None of these is meant
to be glib. You don't say it like this because you've got
brooding down, but because you don't know how else
to say it: you are quite literally *brood*ing. All this aside,
I simply want to address the bone-dry hard-print shape
of it. Brood looks like it is. There is a graphic gravity to
it, holding the letters together, making them a body—a
space—where the convexities of convention converge
with shivering content. That is to say the medium is
the message. But I wrote it like that for want of v's—
of vertex, two lines converging, and the two-front teeth
vibrating on your bottom lip are a charge that connects
one thing to another, and that's what I'm talking about
here. Involved—evolved—continuity of the word gone
to bits.Because if, let's say, your body, your space, were
bathed from birth in words as belief, figures as literal,

stories straight from Mother Mary's teat, dying the yarn of
your cells their otherworldly blue and blood red and wool
white, verses coal- burned into your tongue's groove, now
long emptied of what they were meant to mean, what do
you do with these words, their raveling, warp and woof
of you, undone words that don't go, they dwell in you
and you brood on them, these words, they buzz eternal,
a mouth over water. Here one learns to spell stories like
homonyms. Same shape, different stuff. The word is read
left to right one letter at a time. The characters are the
story. True to *brood*, I can see a stooped but dignified (and
perhaps unhappily bald) figure wandering from b to d....
The drifter enters the space, he slumps down against a
bare trunk, a hunched and hollow bulge:

b

(just see it, don't sound it)

*He himself went a day's journey into the wilderness, and
came and sat down under a juniper tree: and he requested
for himself that he might die.... And as he lay and slept
under a juniper tree, behold, then an angel touched him,
and said unto him, Arise and eat. And he did eat and
drink...*
putting forward, with graphic reluctance, his walking
staff:

r

(slightly hooked at the top)

...only to slump down once again and crawl into a hole:

o

pulling the interiority over himself. *And he came thither
unto a cave, and lodged there; and behold, the word of
the Lord came to him, and said unto him, what doest thou
here, Elijah?* He mopes and gropes his way out, but he
does not exit; he looms in the threshold, in the moan wide

o

*...And, behold, there came a voice unto him again, and
said, What doest thou here, Elijah?* It's clear he can't

hold this moping note forever. The man verily hikes up
his skirts and departs from the dwelling of his agogic
glooming, to here, the end of the word, where he clasps
his mantle on a boy at the plough, the wooly heft coming
down round his shoulders with a hard thud:

duh

(say it)

and there's nothing left to do but let go and get up and go
thence.... *Then he arose, and went after.* Because that's
just the way it is, at the end of brood.

Treehab

"Uh, can you guys tell me which way is Seattle?"

We're in the Arizona bush, about a hundred miles from the nearest convincing town. There are no roads here. Eight of us are squatted on the ground, our limbs freckled with wood shavings as we dully carve and carve whatever's lying around. The boys beautify sticks with which to poke each other.

The man who wants to know just popped out from behind a tree. Really. As his laugh booms his full beard comes alive like some kind of facial beehive. A straw hat makes a wide orbit around his head, tailed with two gray-streaked braids. He wears a spacious muumuu.

No one is alarmed. This desert is enchanted with kindly whacko folk on walkabout. But this man also wears a woven basket on his back. He says the word *food*. In a snap, midday inertia is thrown to the wind. As the teenagers jump up and converge ant-like on the bearded one, my fellow wilderness guide and I hang back to share a look of relief. We've been expecting this man for days. It's been the static word on the walkie-talkie. And though Skyler and I are "Paraprofessionals," as our work badges weirdly certify, we get hungry just like the little guys whose parents or court orders sent them out here. Dave, the man standing in billowy flowered fabric like a 3-D picnic blanket, has PB&Js stowed in that papoose of his.

"Hell yeah!" voice-cracks the first boy to get his grimy hands on the loot. The rest move in with more force, resurface, hold up Ziplocks triumphant. Not just soggy PB&J sandwiches, but to each, a freaking cookie. We retreat to the shade with our kill. Caloric perks like this one are rare and never random. The PB is a pacifying agent, sticking tongues to mouths that might otherwise be inclined to make a racket about how we haven't moved from this stinking spot in almost a week. Normally we'd be hiking sunup to sundown. The boys don't know that we're waiting on vans to transport us to another area in Tonto National

Forest some fifty miles away. It's coming up on mid-summer and time to migrate to where it's cooler—an adjective that means, with Arizonan inflection, a lick less than hellfire. What the boys also don't know, and what Skyler and I know only vaguely, is that these vehicles should have shown up days ago.

It's not unusual for us to be in the dark out here. We go with the flow. But the fact is, we're stagnating in our own sewage. There are only so many places on this small stream-side bank to bury your shit. And the heavy rains will not let bowels be bygones. We would pick up and move downstream but there are other groups. Groups with girls, which the boys must not get wind of. The boys are constantly bickering. They've eaten most of their food packs. Bored. Hot. Bored. Stick-twiddling. Oh hey! an empty beer bottle. Bored. Smelly.

Dave tips his hat in farewell and makes for the creek. "The world is round right?" He languidly saunters, halts, swivels, goes the other way. Calls back, "So I'll get to where I'm going eventually!"

One boy farts. Another calls out, "A-flat, dude!" The gnats buzz and the trees hold their peace.

Hunkered down on a log with my mouth spackled shut and ringed with chocolate, a deep sugar happiness spreads to my heart. I realize Dave was not here to pacify only the adolescents. And I drank the Kool-aid.

+

Plants are sugar fiends. And they make it all in-house—the only beings on earth that are self-self-subsistent, farming food in their own bodies. We're all familiar with their light diet—photosynthesis for us has become an old-school diagram on memory's dusty chalkboards. Yet this superficial familiarity has sapped plants of their gravity. When each breath is given to us silently, seamlessly, we forget the benefactors, the beneficent factories of conditions favorable to life. Photosynthesis runs this planet. We partake of it, directly or indirectly, with every swill of air and drop of liquid, with every single bite.

It's complex. We're still unspooling the ways plants spin threads of air into substantive sugary gold. We're taught that they rustle up a meal by throwing together splashes of sunlight and carbon dioxide, a dash of water, a peppering of minerals. These are facts, whereas it's becoming clear that plants are worlds, teeming with endlessly intricate and interdependent processes.

For centuries it was believed that plants ate dirt, and that this was how they acquired their heft. But in the mid-17th century, a Flemish chemist decided to meticulously measure the mass of soil used by a plant as it grew. He found that the soil contribution to biomass was totally negligible. Some of it came from water, but most came from carbon dioxide. A plant grows largely by substantiating the intangible.

+

We teach the kids to spice up the monotonous food packs with desert plants. Once you look past the land's red austerity, you see greens waving all around—*Pick me, pick me!* Kick of wild mustard, tingly juniper, small, hard squaw berries that tang like Lemonheads, and, if you have the patience to sand off its spines, prickly pear fruit will blow your parched mind: neon wet sweetness with a kiwi-like bite. The boys this week are all about mugwort. They stuff pockets full of it, like wadded cash, to steep later in hot water. Mugwort has flavored drinks since the early Iron Age, treated ailments in Asia for millennia, travelled in the soles of Roman sandals to guard feet against fatigue. But of this rich tradition, our teenage pilgrims are unwitting partakers. One boy heard from another boy who got it from a TrailWalker that mugwort gives you "trippy" dreams. A seed I planted at the beginning of the week. Skyler and I crack smiles at the nightly scene of high- school boys binge-drinking tea. The boys report crazy awesome dreams.

We don't eat meat out here. This is not on principle. There's no talk of eating animals as unnatural or inhumane.

Because, if you wanted to get into the nitty-gritty of what is natural, eating plants is technically outside our human limits. Not one of our human enzymes can digest plant matter. We rely wholly on friendly bacteria in our guts to break down the polysaccharides in plant cell walls. Without these inner aliens, we would have no access to the nutrition growing all around us. Something about this seems perverse. Going back to the Fertile Crescent, greens have been the face of our self-subsistence, growth of our civilizations. What would it mean to know that the food which has allowed humans to cultivate and colonize the world depends, in turn, on the worlds of aliens colonizing our human bodies? It would seem foreign relations are at the heart of humanity. This is at the root of all plants.

+

Eh, meat sneaks in a bit. Sometimes on its own six legs.
What did you just spit out of your mouth!
One of our boys is staring at me wide-eyed, jaw unhinged. He's somewhere between laughing and gagging—the sweet liminal space of ANASAZI.
"Was that a bug? That was a bug." He looks around at the other boys. "Tell me you guys saw that."
But the moment passed only between he and me, and the bug I tongued. "Try it," I say. "It's walking your way now."
He won't today. But he will, he will.

It took me a while to warm up to grub candies, too. Now I can't resist. I have much gusto for cinnamon bugs: slow, dumpy insects who, if popped live inside your mouth, defensively spray from their bum a cinnamon blast that dwarfs Big Red. The impulse to exist has a burn to it. I savor the flavor but not the bug, which can be gently spit into one's palm and sent back on its scuttlesome way. The tongue buzzes pleasantly numb for some fifteen minutes.
Other critters we cook or fry. We eat only what meat we can catch in our small hands—bug bite proportions. Select ants,

crickets, modest crawdads. In the desert it is wiser to shed than acquire: hoarded manna rots. So we stick to the bugs and plants and stay light on our feet. Besides, plants are gracious to beginners. They take our dim tastebuds by the hand: a taste of sweet is a sign of carbohydrates, and keeps the immune system smooth; sour signals astringency, good for the urinary tract and inflamed tissue; bitters, like dandelion greens, are tonic, and coax digestion; spicy warms and moves the body's circulation; calcium is in the chalky; nutrients in the salty. Plants use a vigorous vocabulary. As if they wanted us to gather their meaning.

The kids are wary at first. They don't want to put weird, veiny, raw things in their pie-holes molded to cookie-cutter geometries. They don't want to "get sick." You take plants slow, we tell them. Small. Take just a pinch of any plant. Place it on the tip of your tongue. Chew for two to three minutes. Concentrate. What is the taste at the front of your tongue, and what is the taste at the back. Sit with it. You'll learn the actions of the plant. Taste is a muscle. Coming from a diet tongue-tied with the decidedly sweet or salty, the ability to recognize subtle differences in taste takes time to tone.

Why does it matter? Why dig into the nuances of tastes-like-dirt? To my mind, for the intuition it muscularizes. Plants teeter on healing and toxin. Poison is only a matter of degree. In this way, plants leave room for error, for play: jungle-gym good and evil. We play rough out here, and the bruises and broken skin and bellyaches and ankle sprains begin to constellate into bearings. You get a feel for which stones can hold your weight, and which will turn under you. True learning, like wilderness, is transgressive. And here, as before, learning plants is the fundamental transgression: forbidden fruit; desert exile. Ingestion; expulsion. In the Amazon, where plants are considered teachers, vomiting from vile herbs is called "learning." The shaman, a *purguero*. While our Western culture strives to instill ideas, Wilderness culture seeks to *purge* them. Learning can be a powerful emetic.

I'm lying belly-up under a big old sycamore. The last hooks of light have caught on its peeling scales, its steely green-gray bark, now a near cathode glow. Can a tree beam? It does, it is.

For now I'm down here on the ground because I'm in pain. I'm brought down low to the base of me and this tree. I think temporary fits of physical discomfort are the body's way of exercising hope, which, if left solely to the mind, gets flabby and detached. Headaches make me a different person. More forward-looking than on my clearest days. More meekly receptive than when I'm in top form. More real with the past, more situated in the moment.

These chronic headaches are a gift to me from both sides of my family; a souvenir from brain surgery; my vast inheritance from the desert. When I enter the borders of the middle of nowhere with my group, I know that the first days will be spent in the consciousness-melting magma-spewing pith of my skull. It starts: dehydration trips me from behind; heat remixes the body like an egg beater. At the front of a line of trudging teenagers, a human head implodes.

My head. It's dead of night now. Inside my headache I think about how it hasn't always been this way. In the yester-realities of popsicles and pharmaceuticals and air-conditioning, I could stand up straight and speak in full-on English—at the same time! From down here that life looks like a miracle. The headache pressures me further along its blazing trails. I circle to a familiar signpost: It Will Be That Way Again. The headache is finite. But, in pain, I press the headache, You will end? *Without a doubt*, thumps the headache. *You know how this goes. Now, sit with me.* And like that the headache constrains me to the moment. We don't move a muscle. I'm so limited a whole new field of action opens up to me. I am being in the dark. I am a rabbit hole falling down itself. Spasm fastened.

It's daylight. I'm gazing levelly at the gold loops shooting out plasma-like—cross-hatch creases and cratered pores—from my sun-burned skin. Arm hair. Whoa, I drawl in the slow voice of my headache. Here before me, my skin is a hotspot of explosive events, every follicle a microflare. Whoa. How have I been so blind?

The headache says, *Close your eyes now.* The pulse in my thumbs is huge beyond belief. They are bullfrogs vibratoing each to each. There. A flare in my thigh. Thrums in the bottoms of my feet. A throb between butterflied pelvic bones. I am silently lit up inside my headache. And the future's never looked so bright. In time I will be my old self, and I will know it as sublime. On headache time, my body is a pain-poised world of waiting. A wholly different animal: actively vegetal.

+

Plants operate on a time scale many worlds apart from ours. If we could adjust our eyes to their rhythms we would see active creatures as sophisticated in behavior as animals. As it is, the activities of plants go largely unnoticed by people and our bipedal drives-by. We think of trees as stationary. The truth is, a tree bent by a storm or landslide will go a long way towards righting itself again—you just won't know it till the next year, or five or ten down the road. All the while the tree is busy responding in its own way, growing more and chemically stronger cells on the lower side of the trunk, eventually causing it to stretch and bend upward. These deposits in trees are called "reaction wood." Reaction is right. It's becoming clear that plants are not scenery, not passive entities at the mercy of other forces. They use light, water, gravity, vibrations, chemicals, temperature, predators and allies to inform and modify their way of being in the world. Right here, all around, but existing at a time scale many orders of magnitude slower than ours, plants are wielding light and knowledge.

It's a shift in view. Take it slow. Stroke a pea tendril. It will start to curl. Though, you'll notice, if the plant is chilled, the response won't occur. Take it easy. The memory of your touch remains in the plant. As soon as it warms up, the tendril will curl as if you just stroked it. Plants don't forget you out there. They hold your breath, give it back to you. They grow around your presence. The ceaseless spiraling of stems, roots, and tendrils was meticulously described by the Darwins, who concluded that these oscillations were a plant's response to light, gravity, and other stimuli. Circumnutation, it's called. Research still can't tell us exactly why or how plants curve like they do. Maybe, some said, the perception of gravity on a displaced tip causes the plant to overshoot in the other direction, and so on, creating a spiral. But it's been observed that plants spiral even in outer space. Plant spiraling is now thought to be dependent on internal, not external, causes—the coiled roots you unearth, a visible manifestation of a cell's intrinsic rhythms. It curves, it centers, it touches itself—each plant an introvert.

+

These boys are bipedally impaired. Rocks, branches, and bumps derail their struts. Skyler teases them, "Gentlemen, welcome to the world of uneven ground! No virtual terrain out here." You can't blame their awkwardness. Human habitats are built for a body to get along on cruise control. The boys will gradually get a grip, and it will be a marvelous sight to behold. The desert is a bang-up cure for disembodiment. It calls forth a sort of tactile self-awareness that can only be described as "at home."

Nighttime is part of the transformation. Nighttime helps them unfold. Maybe it's the cover of dark, or the glow of the fire, that makes people more expansive, more soft. This week the group has strung up their shelters side by side in a circle around a single tree. One trunk of branching boys. They've done this so they can all tell stories lying on their blankets. When I joined the circle the other night they begged for one ghost story after another. Some of the tales I told are said to have happened out here. This wilderness—an intersection of Indians, cowboys, Mormons, fugitives—has a fat cache of lore. They want to hear again about the weird lights in the sky. The grim Skinwalkers. The ancient ruins up on the mesa and the sound the wind makes up there. They want to be scared silly.

As they wish. I faded from the circle, got down on the ground, a serpent in the grass. When I came up on the boy with his back to me, when I popped out with a harpy screech, he freaked so hard he jumped up and ran in circles around the fire. And when he had calmed down: "Will you do that again?"

"How can I surprise you when you ask for it?"

"Just... please. I promise to be scared."

Nighttime has a way of making good on impossible promises.

In the desert I developed a taste for darkness. Night hiking. When I was out here as a teenage hostage, we would rest during the lug heat of the day, then set out after dark, when the stars splattered the black sky, like spilled spacetime milk. I was distressed the first time my TrailWalker told me this was our plan. Night was no time to navigate a world stitched with cactus spines. But then we started moving. I was entranced by the way I could see just enough to take my next step. The landscape took on a metallic sheen, as if we were treading the negative of daily reality. Over the course of those months, my body absorbed the darkness like cream on chapped skin. I couldn't know until I went home that I had become such a night lush. For weeks, the tiniest, faintest light would trigger me awake. My sister flipped on the bathroom light down the hall, and I was up on my feet at full alert. Light could stunt as much as it empowered. I started sleeping face down.

+

Desert plants are dark photosynthesizers. Theirs is a unique night-loving metabolism, called CAM photosynthesis. There are three main groups of photosynthesis in plants, branching off each other, but also evolving and re-evolving independently, like alphabets. In standard photosynthesis, used by 99% of the world's plants, the tiny pores—stomata—open during the daytime to gulp the carbon dioxide needed to make sugars. But it takes energy to get energy. The cost of open-mouth kissing the sun is transpiration. Luckily plants—evolved flirts of micro come-ons and pan-species foreplay—have never been passively amorous. To get around water loss, succulents open their stomata only to the night, waiting for the lower temperatures and higher humidity to exchange gaseous spit.

Whatever the brand of photosynthesis, night is an active ingredient. It's now known that periods of light produce the greatest photosynthetic yield when prepped by longer periods of darkness. The slower chemical reactions carried out in the dark prepare the way for the rapid action of light. Photosynthesis, as it turns out, is not a frolicsome dance of sunbeams and sugar. Plants have a dark side, and a world of growth depends on it.

+

Many of the kids sent out to the desert are little devils. Technically they are clinically depressed, or obsessive compulsive, or drug addicts, or pathological liars, or ADHD, or eating disordered, learning disordered, and all manner of disordered. But labels are forbidden to cross into the wilderness with us. I'm not given any information aside from a plain-Jane name. ANASAZI Foundation is adamant on this point. I'm strictly left in the dark, where growth is made possible.

It's clear one of our boys this week is telling fat lies. But still more obvious is just how much it doesn't matter. "Big talk" just plain can't hack it out here. In the desert, persona is the first fat deposit to burn off. So we let things run their course. If a kid decides to run, we don't stand in his way. We walk with him, as far as it takes for him to realize he's getting literally nowhere. If someone refuses to hike, we sit. It is much more challenging to sit with a sitter than run with a runner. A truth plants bear out in their bodies.

Think of it: without the luxury to flee in search of water or shelter or shade or food, a plant is forced to find the means in itself. Their ability to adapt is astonishing, especially here in the desert, where extremes have called forth green Houdinis of contorted genius. While humans move to where we can make it, a plant mobilizes its makeup, forced to re-form and in-form, without reprieve. Poor sods. Yet, for all our fancy pedalism, we humans are no less impeded. Running away is one mirage the desert exposes. Out here we find we're no more capable of escaping our environment, our brain, our body, actions and upshots, than if our cracked soles were tubers in the hard soil. There's no changing the conditions. You must change your life form.

+

Dave, the generous man in the dress, has been called in to give our little Band an afternoon of Stone Age training in building small animal traps in order to distract us from our own entrapment. "Called in" is perhaps an anachronism. I have no idea how Dave was contacted or transported to our whereabouts. The man doesn't have a phone, and when he gives out his email it's with the promise that he'll check it next year.

Dave's campsite is about a thirty-minute jaunt up the creek from our cozy septic haunt. As we round a red rock corner, we see a modest clearing, encircled with trees, a wickiup on the far side. From this man-nest, Dave appears. Dave is a celebrity among people who don't give an owl's hoot about celebrity. He's the legend no one's ever heard. You know "Wilson"? Tom Hank's best-friend volleyball in *Cast Away*? That was a thing from Dave's life. He was the main consultant for the film. He's lived in lots of places that don't have names; run with a lot of caribou. One time I bumped into him in the city. At the time he was practicing abstinence from pavement. He was barefoot and hopping grass patch to grass patch. That's Dave.

Here he is before us, saying, "And that's why to this day dogs sniff each other's anuses." The boys sit on the ground, captivated by Dave's retelling of this Native American myth, which treats the primordial question of why animals have differently sized assholes—and, beneath the story's skin, why one shouldn't meddle with the proportions allotted by creation.

Dave shoots off in a different direction—twisting his spine, turning his head, spinning in circles. "No matter how I stand to make you see the best side of me, someone is always going to be seeing my fat backside!" He pivots as if on the catwalk, looks over his shoulder, and we get his muumuued rump full-on. "You can never see the whole picture," Dave warns the stinky boys. "Beware of thinking what you see is what is there."

Dave is obviously a man who is tutored by plants. A plant will have you seeing only its still exterior. That's the face it wears. But not ever and not even the most unicellular of us is what it appears. Take a few seconds to make a wish on a dandelion and the world inside its cellular walls will have already shifted radically. Within those walls, fluid is in a constant state of rotation—considerably faster than that of ours and other animals. Without joints and muscles, a plant must move from the very center of its cells. To go in a desired direction, a leaflet sends its ions flowing back and forth, changing its cells from turgid to flaccid, its leaves opened to closed, downward to upward—green wings beating. Plant cells work much like micro hydraulic pumps. Its base flaccid, the leaf moves skyward. To go back down, it holds its cellular water: turgor returns. It can do this faster than you can do most anything. Flexing its ions, our plant strong-arms its way to the sun.

I relish that a plant gets its strength not from a skeleton but tiny cell walls, sturdy enough to make paper, ropes, a bench, your house.

+

There's a pile of bones, antlers, and stones at the center of our loose circle of bodies. Dave has brought hacksaws and files for us to create something out of the materials he's gathered. "A gift," he says, "for another. Because the best something is made with someone in mind."

I'm hacking away at a bleached-out hunk, attempting to

make a bone awl. I can't think of many people who will want this gift. I idly look over at Skyler, and find he is looking at me, as he files a piece of antler into something that could be a passable keychain dangly, if all else fails. But I know it wants to be a ring.

Skyler and I have kissed. It was our second night with the boys. Headache Day Two. I was attempting to drink a canteen's capful of creek water every thirty minutes. Two caps down, and I popped my head out of my tarp and upchucked a liquid arc into the dirt. "She even pukes hot," I heard one boy say. They were all squatted outside my shelter, around the small fire. A vomitous female was the most action these boys had seen in weeks. Another boy offered to heat me up some mullen tea. We'd taught them well. But we also wipe our bums with that fuzzy mullen innocuousness. And right then I didn't want a plant; I wanted isolated drugs. Drugs! With impossible names I couldn't pronounce so I could believe they knew better than me, than mullen, than juniper, than sage. I had two emergency Excedrin tucked in my pocket. I swallowed. They came back up, wasted. I meekly accepted the mullen.

It helped some. Around midnight Skyler woke me up to tell me, ironically, that I didn't need to wake up. He'd cover for me. As the adults in legal custody of this Band of lost boys, we're supposed to provide 24-hour care. That means taking shifts throughout the night. More often than not the sky stirs more than the bodies, making it the most lively candidate for conversation. Talking to no one but everything makes sense in the desert. Skyler was talking to me. Giving me a capfull of water. I was feeling astronomically more alive. Boldly I took a full swig from the canteen, let the chill trickle down on my chin, and soon enough, I was swapping full coherent sentences with the shadow crouched outside my tree-hung shelter. It started to drizzle again and the shadow materialized half his body under my tarp. Tinks to thuds to thumps. It was really coming down now. There was no lull in the rain, and the talk never let up.

Storytelling is a tendril, with hairs so sensitive it starts everything twining round each other at the slightest touch. Skyler and I weren't touching yet, but laughing breaths were furling the space between us, inching us inward. By the sixth hour of stories, he had moved from outside shadow to border form to the body next to mine. At 1 and 3/4 inches an hour, we were moving at the speed of bamboo. And so it felt organic when he put his mouth to mine, the last sibilant of the night.

Whatever you are—a man, a stone, a tree—touch is about electricity. Plants know as well as I do when they're being touched. Though the sycamore that held the shelter over us does not have nerves or contracting muscles, the electrical pulses caused by physical stimulations create actions in the tree's body that are eerily similar. A plant's cells, when stimulated, initiate changes in ionic conditions that put out an electric signal, which travels from cell to cell, just as it does in our bodies, and coordinates a response. The truth is that many plants are more sensitive to touch than we are. The airy weight of a string is enough to send a burr cucumber winding its limbs around a nearby object. Our tactile sensitivity wouldn't know such a string if it hit us over the head. Branches swaying in the wind feel the rush. Leaves can feel whether your touch is hot or cold. Supportive or threatening.

A plant feels its world—the wind, the storms, the prods of animals, prickles of insects—and grows to meet it. In turn, the plant grows differently for being touched. In fact, it's been found that simply handling a mustard leaf causes a rapid change in the *genetic makeup* of the plant. A poetic fact humans have long felt: being is fundamentally transformed by touch.

Under that rain shelter, then in sunlight, then beyond desert, in the city, across the country, on foreign couches and under wool blankets, from bored winters to barefoot road trips, long-distance phone calls, silence, sarcasm, ending, and not letting go, and ending again, finally, and forgiving—he and I will grow different for touching.

Here, this is the wilderness, the world outside walls. Contact comes with the territory. It happens, looking up as I stretch awake, that I see the leaves of a sycamore waving over me, and my hair stands on end: *We are here just like you*. This house is alive. The difference between waking up to a plaster ceiling or to animate branches is the difference between atoms and cells; objects and beings; utility and relationality. There is no passive touching in nature. No using without impressing. It messes with your brain, in a trustful way. There. You feel it—the electricity—even if you don't know from where or what or why.

Two lovers pause in a wood as an aside by a stream & touch palms.

Trip Down Happy Valley

He and I are buckled in a borrowed mini-van on an all too familiar
highway in Happy Valley, very much Utah, where all roads lead to
a wedding reception, and he and I have made the trip and dressed
the part, he the Best Man and me his Uneasy Girl, and Oh Lord
this State is eerier than ever and it's a fact—cruise control is an
emotion—like a niggling you've left the oven on a continent
away, so that my throat is fisting, chest gagging, and he offers
a far-off You Alright and I give a flat Yeah Ok, even as my eyes
swell, now spill, and he says What, and I spew Hoo, Hoo, Hoo,
mammoth sobs, all the flaring holes in my face struck up like a
feral choir, and he's going What Is It, and his voice is a whole
other human away, which is It exactly, so I just say I Can't Be
Here and he says Babe I Don't... but I can't hear past my head
slopped to my hands, and any word he says will be the definition
of too little, so I wipe my snot and say instead How's The Driver's
Side and he says Um Good But There's A Governor On It So,
A Governor I ask, Yeah A Governor You Know Like, A Govena
I go, Gov'na he goads, all cheesy English accent, and like that,
one-second zero-to-sixty I'm shot from my head and lodged in
my side—a full-on bloody laugh—swinging rib to rib to slang out
a ruddy luscious Ha Ha! whole Heeheehees, suddenly impossible
to exaggerate, are coming out of my body like immaculate babes,
amnesiac bursts, and he laughs with me as I'm wiping the hell
out of my eyes, and that's when the really unreal thing happens,
when I cinch up in glee-knots, arm reaching for his, and my foot
must press something out there because the glove compartment
yawns open automatic, so processionally slow, so mechanically
self-pleased, so manfully intentional, as one gearing up his jaw
for the first bite of heroic sandwich, but so in excess of that as to
be something else, that I am no longer making a hee and a hee but
being heaved, my body a thing Laughter does, like a great mother
lung, where each breath is a he and I, he and I, until choked up with
joy not to be believed I look to him, my eyes wet and desperate as

I make out Make The Face Of The Glove-Thing When It Opens, which is a precise request like prompting the familiar telling of an old tale, and the need does feel exact, in fact crucial, but I have no idea what the Face would look like, and this is the test, to make the right answer where none existed before, and that is when he veritably swerves the van with A Face I Have Never Seen, like an itch and a scratch in one, and I am relieved as if I had been shown the world ending, the dissolve of the insoluble—he and I mercifully far-gone from words—yet, we both must hear it: the deep-bellied sadness that such a nothing could be so funny, laughter like a rumbling downshift to a gear of low consolation, laughter like there's a gov'na on us, mile after mile limiting our speed, but that's the cry talking again, and so he and I howl down the way not nearing and not knowing which place, the head-ache or the side-ache, is the house he and I live in when the van stops.

Piss On Heartsick

I am a recreational urban urinator. What started as an emergency has since bloomed into intimacy, for cities of 8 million people are not kind to girls with bladders the size of walnuts, so that such a girl has a decision to make: to potty-dance through life, or to engineer a certain cat-sharp awareness of her surroundings—the dark corners, closest parks, the widest bush, the unlikely, barracky, or abandoned. Originally from the exposed, scant-shrubbed desert, I had a knack for sleuthing out coverage. Yet it remained a craft of last-resort, a tight-spot art. Nothing to be cultivated for its own sake. No, it wasn't until last year—winter, heartbreak—that I suspected I wasn't just taking care of business. Pissing openly was doing something to me.

Living in a hard-assed city has only made the surrender more crucial. It happens that there is something about making your body small and low that lays claim to something big and old. I'm not talking about that manly genre of urinating in sweet nature. I mean pissing against the jagged nature of a city, where to make a body vulnerable to its environment is to subvert its environment. You are literally the flesh among steel, the fluid in the gravel, a crack, if you will, in the system. You are a woman, and your body has ever been unstoppably itself. It has been bloody and pissy and bloated in turns, and it fills you now with wonder to let yourself go, right through the cracks of the gum-pocked cement and into some softness of deep-down dirt. And if it is dark out, and there are black tree branches wiring the sky, and a distant rush of cars like a cold river, and maybe a moon, like a flap of skin that makes you suck in your breath, then, on those nights, with my naked backside seated on air and riding a breeze, I feel as if the world is pleased with me. Pissing is not a choice, but here I have chosen to make it part of something beyond square walls, to look carefully around and up and down and side to side to get down low as a prayer and be this body as honestly as I can. I always look first. Left right left sky dirt. As if my body is a child I've taken in hand to cross soundly to some other side, and you passing by, I don't want to cause you to harm me and I don't want to harm you, so I do it deftly, alertly, no derring-do, no up-yours. I respect you, stranger. You are part of the secret orientation of my pissing, along with the trees and the shadows and the buildings. And it is from this my small bare place among you that the feeling arises that I have done alright. The rush comes. I am pleasing in the sight of the world that hides me.

I saw a man's penis reflecting the daylight in Riverside Park, him looking me bold in the face, and disgust and rage flared like a sunburn under my skin. You piss standing up? Against a wall, whatever, whenever, anywhere, and without a second thought? I am not impressed by the urinating man. Because, if I didn't get low, get small, get private, the piss alchemy wouldn't happen, and I don't know how much you've had to relieve yourself in cities, but I'll tell you not so long ago I was dying in Central Park, after dark, deep fall, my legs tracing endless loops going nowhere, because I knew what would happen if I ended up somewhere. He would not be there. So I become slippery around places, taking back-alleys of reality, roaming other times like my own ghost come back to haunt me, so that when I touched a tree it was a wormhole to another tree I hugged with luxurious hope years ago—20-years old and in love half-way across the world—before I knew bitter and sweet in the cellular nuclei of my body, that is, before loving you, before losing you, and these two trees are not connected by anything but me, and I can't bear the burden of being this node of bones where past and future fail each other. How the past would die if it knew how I live. How the future mourns.

How I stumble like a tumbleweed of snarled sobs. And believe me this girl can cry like she pisses: anywhere, openly, pit-deep and displacing dirt as she goes, you can feel the steam off her eyeballs. You can smell her murk. This night I got down, knees and forehead to the cig-butt mulch of the city, behind a bush, where many others have preceded me with their own business—I catch their dank life and body leaks on my clothes and in the sticky silk of my nostrils—but these are not my concern. My business here is this: to be dirt before what I don't know. Because I don't know, I don't know, what else is mighty enough for this bodily prayer except what is too mighty to definitely be. So I get low, because it smells and it feels like the threshold where words and fears and hope s come to decompose.

And it's mad work to cut him off, nerve by nerve in the seasons-dense patterns of him in my body, and there, where he sprawled out for a king's nap in the grass of my mind, left a smoosh of neurons in the shape of his hard man body. That person who is so twined with my thinking that every thought frays me as I tweeze him out. And tonight it's too much for me, I could just die, should just die. But first, I had to piss.

I set my blurred sights on a tree. The tree was a man. I quickly veered the other way, headed for a true gingko. Further, further, near the mud cakes by the duck pond, muck and brush leaves all around, I let down the pants that have begun to sag off my hipbone sadness. When the stream hits the small stones and soil, it's a self-sauna of my own spice-hot Phosphorus, my insides like incense before my face, my Nitrogen, my Potassium, my pressurized Helpless, and it helps the flowers grow. I watch the flow curl around me, feel it seep under me. That gut-deep piss-dirt scent, like the spit and mud enough to open the eyes of a blind man. A switch goes on. Just like that. *Oh*. I stand up and step back. Breathe again, and say in a voice I've not heard in too long, girl, you are an old soul, maybe an endless soul, so what's your big idea to get through this one?

There was a day, a sunny not quite spring day in New York City, and it was my morning to Run & Be Free, to take by the balls those 6,7,8 miles—my bare thighs thunderously numb with cold and tears whipping back into the small holes of my ears—and man do I need that, like bread and water and the warmth of his palms on the small of my back. On this morning, my stomach said, No. But it was my Run & Be Free Day, so I ran, and demanded the Free keep pace. About 3 miles in it was clear my body would not do this no matter what I did. There was a demon pain inside me clawing to get out. But I said I'll just go 1 more mile and turn around. Surely I can do that. No. I started looking for a toilet. Nearest one 15 blocks away, the gardener said. Surely I could. I could, oh no, I could, oh my, oh no, shit, shit. I started looking for a bush, staggered steps. No bushes, no, no. This can't happen, because it can't, I can't shit myself in the middle of the city, that would be impossible, unthinkable.

Wh-what did you do? said the friend I was telling this story to, my arms and legs wrapped around her body and my mouth to the back of her neck blowing warm story air down her spine. I massage her crabbed hands. Black desert rains slap us silly. She is shaking up and down, out of control, can't control, and she is a very self-controlled person, who I had to strip down ass-naked out of her layers of wet clothes and wrap a tarp around her slippy seal skin and get all of me suctioned on her like a starfish. And we got in this mess all because we wanted to drop our shit. Two crazy heartsick girls who asked the desert to kick our ass to freedom: we left behind our sleeping bags, our food, our warm clothes. Set off. We prayed boldly, we dropped heavy stones off cliffs. Howled for heaven and earth to hurt us all the way to healing... and then she got hypothermic.

Well, I tell her, somewhere between home and a toilet, time stopped. I felt all of me jerk still. I didn't dare breathe lest something come loose. It was a surreal moment, as I watched the city-goers walking past me, right up against me, and I knew—with a rare and total clarity—that in all the world there was no other choice but to here and now shit myself. And what is heartbreak and loss and incontinence but the moment when the unimaginable gets exclusively real. And so I shat. I let go absolutely. It was messy and gnarly and streaming down to my right ankle, and Lord knows I was wearing no underwear but the tiny betraying one of my running shorts good as cheese cloth. It happened. And then I turned around and started walking the 3 miles home. And I was, right there, I realized, elated. I couldn't stop smiling, because in a way it was such a wild relief to have no options. A lady walked past me and covered her nose, and I felt myself hold my head higher. Because what has more concentrated force than the body that is a walking breathing stinking mass of nothing-else-I-can-do!

Will you. Sing for me? I just. Need singing, she said. Well I'm exquisitely tone deaf. I sing for no one, but I damn sure sang for her, belted out in the storm every verse of Boots of Spanish Leather, and then an encore, because there's nothing else to be done right now but have it all out there, all on the table, chills and dirt shimmying down our skins, menstrual blood seeping through (when it rains...), no food to move our bowels, but if we shake enough with the rain we might just dislodge something— laughter, she is laughing at the story, at the shit running down my legs in New York City, and one day we will laugh at this sopping bloodknot we are. Hell, we already are. Laughing in our lost liquids, we are pure.

And honestly I'm not sure why there isn't more talk of the ties between love and bowels. We talk about love and food, but not what happens after you put the goods in your mouth. They go down, down, into the hairy netherworld, long and tender and full of transformations, and I can barely eat these days out of hunger for you, and I think of my Mother, how, back when she still had most of her viscera, her love life revolved around her intestines, so unruly and troublesome she had to strategize where and when she went out with lovers, and it's so hard to let yourself go, to expose that soft fleshy middle where we are helplessly broken down, and I think of the time in the beginning, when I was your idol, dream girl, etc., and I was lying on my back on the ground and you stood on my stomach and I squeezed every muscle to hold you up and— pfoof—I farted. And oh the look on your face, your blue eyes like crushed diamonds and you dying laughing, and I said, When you step on me what do you expect? And how can you love without stepping on each other, and if you are to hold the weight of the other with your tenderest parts you had better flex every muscle, and Lord knows that creates its own winds. I thought, There's more where that came from, I'm no dream girl, and I've been an idol before and I know how they fall, and how no one waits at the bottom, and I told you to curb your worship and hold the tongue of your promises, because they don't stay in the mouth forever, they go down, down, and all things must pass through the low places, but knowing that is not to gain an ounce of control, and oh God did I fall hard, I full-on fell until here I am just me, *just me*, down where the unimaginable gets exclusively real.

I'm sick, really sick, my heart reeks to high heaven, and there's nothing I can do, can't hold, can't stall, can't soothe, sorry can't wait for a better moment. I give in and let it all power out, with respect for you, for myself, for the heartbroken earth pissing oceans of tremendous bottomless fragility, and sometimes I feel it, when I'm filthy through and through with my own blackblue heartguts: the world is pleased with me. I am doing human alright. There is an unlovely love that lives at the bottom and you can flush it out of sight or you can get low and give it up for the flowers. And the orientation of my heartspill is towards you who can't see me, but I bare and feel and smell and know I'm real and that there are growing things here, unbearable growing things. And I know because, later that day that I shit all over myself and beyond myself, I met up with a friend, and you know the first thing she said to me? *Oh my God, you're glowing! Are you in love?*

Dirt Tea

1

Germ is slur for microbe.
Your own slush and guts, flesh
and crud—your Mama, the
first germstress, you lucky dog,
who passed through her veil of
vaginal wildlife, coating you
like live armor, like ingenious
fur, to capture your Father's
blessing, to prosper your tiny
humanness in its immense
otherness, you whose human
cells are outnumbered 10 to
1 by the bacteria who let you
live and feel and think, and
think you're the human shit,
while your germ mass wildly
outweighs your gray matter.
Why would you plug your
nose?

2

You piece of dirt, fall down
and feel it. Skin your knees on
piles of kin, let your humuses
kiss, pet, bleed on all of this
is you. Would you bandaid an
ocean?
Welcome to the soiled
wholesome world, bugbitch.

3

We are made of star stuff,
we say, born showoffs. How
grand, how expansive. Oh
brother, look down and feast
your eyes underfoot! One
kilogram of soil has got more
microbes than stars in this
galaxy. We are wondrously full
of shit, nebula boweled and
alien skinned: with each step
planets press into our populous
soles, in us and on us, whole
civilizations eat and breathe
and screw and die.

4

Your belly has a couple million
more genes than your parents
could give. Mama gets it
takes a village. Not one of
your 23,000 human genes can
digest the bounteous carbs of
mother's milk, or the green
meat of plants. Only germs
have the touch. Only together
we break bread. For in the
beginning Mother made a pact
with the bugs, long forgotten
in the war on dis-ease, war
calling itself a clean business.

5

We are deathly clean. Post-
fungi sarcophagi, gutless,
gutted, micro necrophiles,
reeking de-stinkly, screening
our microbes like X-rated

chromosomes, washing hands,
plugging smells, bleaching,
sloughing, scrubbing, utterly
rubbing out our raw. Men
would do well to act like dogs:
sniff out exemplary shit to
chow down and gentrify our
gut slums.

6

We'll eat it one way or another.
Fecal transplants are the new
Doctor's orders. For decades
we've been on waiting lists
for liver, kidneys, bowels,
when perhaps a loaned doo-
doo would do. For centuries
vets have been serving shit tea
to sick animals. We are sick
animals. Humility is sticking
the Other's crap up your hole:
Humanity in need of an enema.

7

Oh the Pow! vested in garbage.
Garb aged, worn, mended,
remade, dead enough to be a
thriving something else. Take
me to the land of raw milk and
honey, where the angels speak
black banana, ex cathedra,
excreta, excreta! Mud pies
manna to my waste lands.

8

Take me down to the fine night
soil near infinite in me, where
stampeding beasts toss their
manes in the winds of my gut,
vile and free...

9

Because I was born with a hole
in me. Eight holes, for humans
can't take a hint. We think in
closures. Personal space. But
here is my person peopled
to the nth power: born to die
entryways without end.

10

Can't we be adults about this?
Our bodies do the dirty. To the
gods looking down, I am floors
upon floors of tenants, trillions,
cleaning house, making love,
taking meals, sorting trash,
growing, changing, leaving,
replacing, immigrant beats
pulsing through atom-thin
walls. Holy, holy is the
teeming of my tongue, this,
here, melting pot multiverse
tanging with inner aliens.

11

What I'm saying is in your
soft middle sits a second
genome. A second brain. Your
stomach more than growls;
it speaks straight to the head.
The two are mushy confidants,

frenching cells: the very
thought of eating gets the
stomach juicing, and a troubled
stomach burdens the brain.
Esophagus to anus, an ongoing
pilgrimage. A trail where bugs
change our minds and bowel
is always a movement. The
microbial self: my hand is
others' handwriting.

12
Dear Superorganism,
Your first genome is
irrevocable. Your parents are
sorry. But your microbiome is
a meal away from a different
life. Forgive and flush out your
parents. Bacteria are the most
open-minded tribe on Earth.
Work with them. Your turf is
gardenable, your doors ajar:
catch nature and nurture in the
act! My dear coupling one, be
the germs you want to see in
the world.

Grease Catcher

You're hungry. It's natural. You feel like meat. Rip this page
out. Rip it out and place it on your cutting board. You want crisp
greens and shy yellows and watery reds, too. You don't want to
mess with washing your cutting board in between. That's what
this page is for. It is a disposable membrane separating your raw
meats from your fresh greens. Cut into it. Cut your meat on it.
That's why it exists. There are many reasons to exist. This page
gets this one. Who says? I say, but who am I? I'm someone with
unreliable reasons to exist. I eat meat these days. I eat dead things
to live, which would suggest I see great reason to my existing. It
would suggest I feel more worthy of more. But all it in fact means
is I'm an animal. I don't feel much for animals. But I do say thank
you to plants I pick. And sorry. Some vegetarians I know say
they find animals too much like us. Somehow this is exactly what
fails to make me take them seriously. But plants. Plants have no
interest in playing at us. No eye contact, no wet noses, not a single
winking tooth. They're lightyears past my heavy-handed ways.
Once I got upset at my potted fern and put it in timeout. This was
after I drank a prayer-soaked Amazonian jungle brew to better
know myself and plants but rather fell into a blank spring-less
hole. It hurt my feelings. Sometimes a nameless vine creeps up
and strangulates my spine that I don't know, can't see, not myself
not what grows. It takes a mirror to see your spine. To see your
eyes. And yet a mirror is the furthest distance between your face
and your face. This page does not want to be a mirror. It wants to
be the surface you cut your meat on. And just maybe the meaty
grease will blotch it see-through, like a window, or ill monocle.
Because this window doesn't open, because this monocle has no
eye, here's a prayer for the meat cut hereon, olive-oil-rubbed and
salt-and-peppered. Sorry to not have known you alive. Sorry to
run on what I've overwhelmingly not known alive. And may our
swallows not all be sorry. May this unopening window, this ill
monocle, tossed out with the other scraps and damp gunk, be the

lens through which the bruised arugula and limp chicken skin see each other, and break down, as we break down, with mixed hungers.

Sacred Spirit Medicine: "Sacred Spirit Medicine"

As it is I'm riding the A train, and when I close my eyes a most unsolicited voice addresses me.

Me: So you drank the plant Kool-aid, did you?

Me: When did you start talking to me like I'm not you?

Me: Exactly.

Me: Look, I swallowed a life-altering plant. It should be in my head. Not you—me. You're laughing. What do you know?

Me: The Shaman warned you, you'd just be drinking yourself.

Me: I thought that meant, like, me uninhibited. Me as a plant, through a plant, the primary source. Not me doubled, squared, exponentially just me...

Me: And me.

Me: Stop talking to me like I'm not already way too much you. Like you're not the monologue I was trying to climb out of, up in the trees, out on a limb.

Me: I'm what the tree's giving you. You.

Me: I was already me.

Me: Me.

How did we get here?

He and I are alone on the beach, and it's so dark the ocean and the sky are untellable from each other but for the white crests of the waves, though clearly the crests are not white because nothing could be in this dark, and this dogs me because, then, what color are they? I try to make my eyes new and look. These crests, this sand, like some after-glare of color behind squeezed eyelids. Also the saliva-shiny snarls of water, water snagging on itself, and this makes a color, too. Or I'm just hearing it. Night tilts me further into soundscape, and I wonder about the reverberations of this ear-coloring—how hearing, often called "the spiritual sense," has long been seen as a threat to reason's ascendency. The blind recitation and audition and memorization of listening—those passive, hairy pitfalls of ear canals—all in contrast to the sharp rationality of sight—

I'm relieved when I cut myself off. I'm not thinking like this tonight. No hierarchy of senses, thoughts, interpretations. Tonight I'm bypassing ears and eyes altogether, going straight to internal sense. True vision, true hearing. Thought will not be something I do. Thought will just happen. Simple and pure. Ayahuasca, a 100-proof reality-check direct from the Amazon, will pare me down to what's greater than me.

Like hell it will, says another sense of mine. My bullshit olfactory region, which, despite my most zen intentions, is sniffing up a storm in this scenario. With reason. Where the hell is our Shaman anyway?

My friend next to me shivers. Dave and I are relatively recent inhabitants of New York. When I was told we should meet them ("Who?" Dave asked. "Them," I offered again) at the beach, I was fairly thrown off. A beach? In New York? Dave had a similar reaction. Not a few things seemed shady. But I was going on faith, which requires not a graceful but awkward leap. And lo, here we are, 10 p.m. at Far Rockaway in chill March, a boy from Kansas and a girl from Arizona—or, two adult Mormons about to have their first true "trip."

Our form of transportation is ayahuasca, or "sacred spirit medicine," as it's known back home in the Amazon. A shamanic confection, tonic of cosmogonic insight. "Liquid love," said the particular shaman we're here to meet. And still no sign. I'm so excited, and so tired, my readiness has begun to rot. I've been fasting all day. No one else is here on the unlikely beach to meet us. We find ourselves freezing.

Luckily Michael, the guy who connected me to this astronomic occasion, is given to putting neon lights in the tips of his gloves and twirling them about. After a while Dave and I spy the spectacle down a ways and up on the pier. As we near, Michael appears to wear a halo, his fuzzy dreadlocks catching the woolly yellow of lamplight. He and his friend welcome us with wind-drowned hoots. They're stoned, and merry, and as clueless as we are as to the exact cosmic coordinates of our Shaman. "The Russian spa, last we heard," Michael reports, rechecking his cell. This is when I find out our Shaman is not, as I had imagined during our phone conversations, a big robust brown man, but is, from Michael's description, a hilariously tall and skinny, red-headed middle-aged man of obscure European extraction—possibly the Balkans? His accent has eluded us all.

Five hours after the meeting time our man appears. Praises be, he's brought blankets. He drops the heap on the sand where we're huddled, half-asleep, and powers right into ceremonious hugging. The Shaman takes each of us in turn. When he comes to me he gives what could be the best hug I've ever had—breathing me in like this is the last time we'll ever meet, here, at the edge of ocean, sky, city, minutes away from astronomical equidistance, Spring in its cosmic sense—and he and I, breathing, breathing— but I don't actually know this guy. I feel slightly mocked. Stop, I tell myself. Tonight everything just is what it is.

The Shaman's name is Sandor (pronounced Shan-door). "What door?" I asked the first time Michael told me. After meeting the Shaman in person I wonder if my bad hearing isn't prescient. This giant, man, dude, sage, is nothing short of a portal. He's a mood, a nimbus of relaxed baggy clothing, a patina of smile wrinkles etching the wizened eyes. With a rampant calm he bounds around and rears a space for us to enter, setting up his sound system, spreading out blankets, humming and talking and chuckling as one unbroken song. Shamans are performers after all. As off-put as I at first feel to have this redhead white guy Shaman, I know it's unfounded. A prejudice of false origins. Shaman, as a word, actually comes from Eastern Europe. The shamans were the community healers of Siberia, where mushrooms were their metaphysical morsel of choice. The English lexicon doesn't give us many terms in this tradition, so we've borrowed the one and generically tacked it on to different practices from innumerable regions, the Amazon most especially.

What is a shaman, then, in its traditional sense? Perhaps most importantly—and popularly overlooked—a shaman acts as an intermediary between the human community and the natural world. He's a border dweller. He ensures that there is a proper flow of nourishment, not just from the earth to humans, but from humans back to their environment. A key power of the shaman is his ability to slip out of the perceptual boundaries of his particular culture—boundaries of social customs, taboos, speech and language, constructed values. A shaman is a shapeshifter.

I'm glued on Sandor, watching each movement. He's garrulous in a muted way, perhaps in part because of his slippery accent, and in other parts—ten yards from us—the drown-out of a sloshy ocean. As he twines together a handful of sage, he's saying, not once checking for an audience, "You know when people asked me as a kid what I wanted to be when I grew up I never said rich or famous or a career I wanted. I would always say I wanted to be happy." He chats about the cult of money, of success, of achievement. About freedom from lies we've internalized. He asks us all to rise to our feet, he lights the sage, he waves it till smoking, he starts facing the first of us, tells the small man to stretch his arms out to his sides, he runs the fulsome fume over all the man's body, head to foot, front to back: the Shaman is blessing him. He repeats this slowly and fully with each one of us, ending with Dave next to me. He asks Dave if he will bless him. Dave smiles nervously, then mimics the Shaman's motions, down to the last flourish of running the hand up the spine with a playful whoop.

   Before we'll take the medicine, he says, it's important to go around the circle and voice our intentions. At this point there are eight of us. Excluding the Shaman, only two have taken ayahuasca before, and only once before, they say. These two came together a few hours later than the rest of us, after Sandor even. They look to be in their early forties, foreign, a couple. Cute, I think. The short man to their right might be in his late thirties. He came with the Shaman. This is his first time. He's soft spoken. His intention, he says, is that he'd like to be happy. He smiles without parting his lips and shrugs his shoulders, somewhere between bashful and rueful, and I want him to be happy. The couple say they'd like to feel God's love and know what God would have them do for others. The Shaman adds that we can invite the spirits of others to accompany us. A lot of Jesus, Krishna, exotically consonantal names, family, friends, teachers, and dead ones are invoked. Each list longer than the last. When it gets to me, I give a list of intentions and people I want to join me, which is funny because there is really only one thing I intend, and I forget to say it. I think at one point I said I hoped to feel in love and that I wanted to hear Krishna singing. *What?* My list only stopped short of a unicorn. I'm unsettled by my babble. The anything-goes spirit of this circle feels an awful lot like peer pressure. I'm meaning more than I mean. All I meant was: I want to get out of my head and see a new angle.

   The Shaman's in no rush. He passes around his teasing glass jars full of deep red. Not yet for the taking. He wants us to get to know it. To look the stuff in its liquid eye and give it thanks and love. I do. I want to share a moment with this plant I've been thirstily seeking. I hold the jar between my hands and stare into its cloudiness. The moment doesn't hold. I'm too eager to go all the way. I look at Sandor. Though he's surely the shamanic performer, he's also the rare human who seems to have ceased to exist in relation to audience. His eyes are closed. He's cradling one of the jars against his chest with disarming affection. His lips slip up in a slight smile. Even his repose is kinetic. Less a Buddha, I think,

than a young Saint Nick. A night owl alchemist of secretive glee.
I feel special for being here, a sense I'm critical of. Yet crave. It's
special inside the circle. While I don't exactly feel like I belong,
I do feel like I'm part of something. Which is something. Here
we are warming ourselves together off the beaten path. Here we
are—a staggering fact alone.

How did we get here?

Ayahuasca was a breadcrumb I came upon a year ago after
deciding that life was an animate forest, making me lost but never
alone. I decided this because of one totally anomalous moment
with a plant. What I'm calling a moment was probably about half
an hour in which a queerly exquisite clarity came over me, or
through me, my self-composed eyes momentarily come undone,
and I saw that plants had a rich inner life teeming with generous
gifts and intelligence and communications, which, until then, I
had never supposed in any way beyond the poetic. I was sober,
by the way. The encounter left my way of thinking speechless. A
full inventory of reality would be necessary. What is really going
on? I asked biology, ethnobotany, anthropology; Eastern religions
and traditions and lore. I asked the plants, too, like I used to ask
God. But they were just as perfectly silent. Or I was habitually
deaf. What experiences were possible? Whatever the field or
the book, it seemed to make mention of a particularly spirited
vine: Ayahuasca. I followed the trail, read incredible narratives,
experiments. Here was a plant that *talked*, that is a being, with
things to say—to you.

Ayahuasca is its Quechua name. While *huasca* is the
common term for any species of vine, *aya* is a more slippery
branch of significance: the word means something like a separable
soul. One translation articulates it as aya: soul/dead; wasca: vine/
rope. Which leaves us teetering on an eerie fence. Aya-wasca: A
soul, like life + a vine, like climbing / the dead, like ghosts + a
rope, like hanging.

The translation you go with would seem to matter. Or

maybe there is no either-or in the murk green world. Plants are no sweethearts, I have to remind myself when I slip into making daisy chains with the wonder of them. Awe is not a separable spirit from awful.

The ayahuasca I'm referring to is not a plant, per se. It's a brew, an involved blend with a range of some 100 species. There's the ayahuasca vine, the stem of which is processed into a drink, but the more potent hallucinogenic part is found in its popular companion plant—chacruna—whose leaves are rich in dimethyltryptamine, or DMT. When taken orally, DMT is inactivated by an enzyme in the lining of the stomach. The ayahuasca vine ingeniously inhibits this enzyme, allowing the digestion of all those visions shored up inside. This happy companionship was developed in the upper Amazon we know not how long ago. The ritual use of ayahuasca is the common religious and spiritual trunk of some seventy indigenous branches across Brazil, Venezuela, Colombia, Ecuador, Peru, and Bolivia. Its use is growing among the mestizo population, not to mention tourists and pilgrims, and there is an ongoing argument among anthropologists of whether the indigenous people passed the ayahuasca knowledge to the mestizos or if, in fact, the mestizo population brought it to indigenous groups. When asked who taught them, the people say, again and again, and across languages and cultures, *the plants told us*.

Ayahuasca is not a healing plant. It's a teaching plant. This distinction is a very important one in most traditions. Ayahuasca is not used to take away one's sickness, though it will surely make you purge. Yet, even the intense vomiting and diarrhea have a didactic aspect: *La purga misma te enseña*, they say; vomiting itself teaches you. The value of the plant and the role it plays in its community is to give a person the knowledge she needs to discover what *causes* her sickness, and how to get rid of it. Just as medicines in these shamanic communities are not isolated active ingredients, neither are illnesses isolated. They are relationship based. An ache in the pancreas points to an ache in the pantheon—a body is nothing less than an embodiment of the community, of the environment.

Plant spirits, particularly that of ayahuasca, teach the people how their relationships to each other or the natural world are poisoned, and the way to purge the betrayals. The plant imbues its imbiber with a perspective that will work on her long after it is thrown up and buried. Some say it teaches us that the natural world is wildly communicative, that the plants are singing to us all the time, if we can only open ourselves to their voices.

The psychedelic heyday of the '70s left a thick haze over the study of hallucinogens. Overenthusiastic advocacy of psychotropic drugs burned itself out like so much hash, and no researcher thereafter wanted to touch the soiled connotations of ayahuasca. It was bad science. That is until recently. Studies on psychotropic plants are beginning to grow back in a more serious light. In the past couple of years research has shown successful results in ayahuasca treatment of drug addiction (positive in 2/3 patients), as the concoction offers not simply a chemical reconfiguration but a perspectival reorientation—a process of unlearning and rediscovery. It is also now being used to treat depression in patients dealing with terminal diseases. This vine, they're finding, is no mere quarry of chemicals, but a composite that includes right intention, situation, and setting. And time. That healing is slow and highly involved might be the hardest pill for many of us to swallow. The studies—and ever the shamans—seem to be saying that plants are artists not objects: they work best on us on their own terms and in their own time.

Though ayahuasca is not a "healing plant," there are healing stories of its power—common motifs spanning time, individuals, and traditions. Descending into hell to break through to the light; encountering former or future selves; inhabiting other forms and perspectives; melting into otherness and the universe; and not least, all-encompassing love. A captivating *National Geographic* article recounts the tale of one journalist's transformative experience with the drug while deep in Peru's Amazon. On emerging from her first ayahuasca trip, she tells us, "I discovered the impossible: The severe depression that had ruled my life since childhood had miraculously vanished." This is the article I sent Dave the morning of our own ceremony, as if to say the uncatchable is on our platter tonight.

The article reminded me of a story a girlfriend told me that has never left me. She dealt with depression from an early age. When she was fifteen, she got a particular Priesthood Blessing from her uncle. My friend's uncle placed his big hands on her red-gold hair and said that she would no longer have depression. God said it wasn't needful anymore. This is my friend's story. My friend says the depression left her and it didn't come back. She told me this, I think, to say this can happen to you. Happiness is as real as it is improbable. It can spark from a slight pressure of hands, or from one night of jungle indigestion. I wonder if, on some basic level, happiness itself isn't delight at its own unlikeliness. And so, why not? Why not put yourself in the prayer-oiled palms of an old man? In the clutch of liquified vine? Why the hell not?

I had my doubts. I let the information steep. It would be a while before I would think that ingesting the drug firsthand would be something useful. And even once I decided it was crucial, I couldn't just up and do the damn thing. First, ayahuasca is an exotic recipe; the authentic one is hard to come by. Also, I wanted all the proper ceremonial trappings. I needed a guide, a community— allies to smooth my landing into the inner underworld. Not a party, but a people. Where do you go shaman hunting in Manhattan? I felt helpless. I actually started praying to find the plant. Praying to whom? I didn't know. That's one of the reasons why I urgently needed to get an audience with this ayahuasca. I heard she imparted knowledge mercilessly.

Late Thursday night, talk turns honest with a friend in her apartment. She reads to me from her journal about her ayahuasca encounter while living in India. Her experience is almost painful to hear—I want, with a guttural sort of spiritual lust, her insights for myself. I'm ready, I tell my friend. I'm so ready, I just don't know how to make it happen. My friend does not suffer the hippie. So I know, when she says it, she means business: The *plant* will find _you_. Less than 24 hours later I meet Michael. It's his first time at the _Bhagavad Gita_ discussion group I've been going to for the past six months. He studies religion and psychoactive therapy. In his hands I spy an article on ayahuasca, one I recognize. When he leaves early I chase after him. I tell him why we should talk. Like me, he's been reading up on ayahuasca but has yet to experience it. He wants to. He knows a shaman. We exchange information. I can't believe it (but of course I can). I'm elated. Michael is so elated he gets a tattoo. He shows it to me when we meet two weeks later on Spring Equinox, under some few stars, out on a beach, holed up in blankets, circled about a red-headed Shaman who is also a raw foodist—personally and professionally—and, for apparently far-out (karmic) reasons, really quite wealthy. The sound system he's brought he bought the day of. He's now saying, "Welcome to this most powerful night of the year." He's saying that we're a pocket of consciousness raising, and that right now there are small groups of us gathered and scattered all over the planet. He says, "I'm glad you all made it."

How did we get here?

They say that the first algal scum got its digs into land some 1200 million years ago. They say algae is persistently "simple." From this cellular oneness all plants have evolved, each tree an outgrowth of pure minimalism. The Greek nymph Pitys opted to be changed into a tree rather than deal with the complications of love and life and satyrs just out to get some. "Look: the trees exist," said Rilke. They are unmuddied existence. They _are_, simply. "The clearest way into the Universe is through a forest wilderness," John Muir wrote; and Emerson held, "The creation of a thousand forests is in one acorn." "And this our life," goes Shakespeare, "exempt from public haunts, finds tongues in trees." Plants, it seems to us, are the naked pattern of real life. Innate knowledge, solid being, all sprung from some primeval green cell. The insight ayahuasca promises is not new. It comes from a long line of wholer-than-thou simple cells.

Or it comes from our ideas about them. O the repose of simple organisms! If only we could recapture our innocent origins! It would seem models of life supplied by molecular biology create a kind of nostalgia in our cells. The researchers who call themselves Microscopists, however, tell a very different story. To these occultist minimalists, single-celled organisms, like those that resulted in plants, exist not as a simple code but as an enduring mystery beyond human understanding. In fact, one argument from this field is that cells themselves are ingenious. They are living entities exhibiting behaviors, skills, structure, and creativity much like our own. Single cells are not merely the building blocks; they are the builders. The achievements of multi-cellular organisms, such as trees and humans, are, they suggest, resonances of what a single cell can perform. We're just doing better what cells do best.

Take the amoeba, famously the simplest form of life known to science. This simply isn't true. The amoeba's metabolism, activity, motility, feeding, excreting, and sensing share much in common with our own. Not to mention, no two amoebae are ever the same shape. For centuries humans have claimed as our main distinction the fact that we can use tools, we can craft, build. *Homo faber*, man the creator. But an amoeba—our planet's resident simpleton— could rival our handiwork with its ability to create artificial objects without even the use of hands. A pond water amoeba will spend some of its day finding small sand-grains, gathering them up and cementing them together to form a microscopic home for itself. It lives in a purpose-built shell, delicately constructed by the process of locating, sensing, selecting and arranging minute materials. No easy task. This organism we think of as simple and transparent is actually a master manipulator. Where is pure being when even the algae are busy making constructs?

And messy love. On a cellular level, organisms as seemingly personality-less as protozoa prefer companionship to mere feeding, which doesn't make much sense practically. Courtship for protists is superfluous, and interrupts the vital feeding process. Yet these teeny-weenies, every so often, like to mingle, to inspect each other, and—smooshing together the oral sides of their cells—to embrace. Why? One theory is that they enjoy it. Whatever the reason, even simple green organisms are compelled to pay the price for intimacy. Our soil-smug nymph, Pitys, was sorely mistaken when she thought boarding herself up inside a tree would free her from lover antics.

Much emphasis in biology is placed on networking—each cell a sort of transistor in a larger computer. If only we could map the brain's connections, we say. We'd solve the human puzzle. What clever amoebae seem to point to, however, is that neuronal cells don't just carry out their work between themselves, but within themselves. Life is thinking on every level. So that one must ask, what organism—simple or complex—is cut a break in a world where processing is intracellular in nature? How can we escape complexity? What is that place where things just are? The origins of plant life appear to say—in unicellular unison—Hey don't look at us. We're all coming from someplace messy that was never neat. Victorian textbooks offer a telling taxonomy: the common amoeba, A*moeba proteus*, was known as *Chaos chaos*.

You won't have to think, just let the medicine take care of you, the Shaman told me on the phone in our first conversation. Just let the plant go to your heart. Let go of your stories, your history, and just exist, simply. Being can be effortless.

I was surprised when I last minute invited Dave to the drug ceremony. I met Dave in Church. Or rather, on my way out of it. Dave was a practicing Mormon, yet a true outlier. He and I would take epic walks around the city, talking in our common first language of Mormonism, all the while finding our own fringe dialect: How we didn't believe, how we did, and how to manage on the margins of a religious community that doesn't yet allow room for margins. Out of respect, I never invited him out for a drink. Yet I found myself asking him along for an exotic drug trip. His closest friend had just killed himself a couple weeks before. He was depressed. He wanted a new perspective. When I invited him against reason, and he, against reason, said, "Yes," I thought, with no small measure of self-satisfaction, *This must be an impulse from the Universe,* or, in my native tongue: *this is a Prompting from the Holy Ghost.* This plant is meant to help Dave, just like it's meant for me. Look at this plant, already bringing humans together.

Now, here we are. Out on the blankets on the beach in the fog and only fog in my head, I've rarely felt so isolated. The Shaman has turned on the music. What seemed at first desultory and soothing and all-around ear-tingly has become the bastard child of dying whales and idling flying saucers, as the long deliberate monotones push more on crazy than chakra for me. Dave is right next to me. Without turning to me he says, simply, "I feel depressed."

How did we get here?

For a few weeks there I was moving backwards. Literally, on the sidewalk, in the street, or through parks, even up hills, stairs. Sometimes, while walking in a citizenly forward direction, I would turn myself about without warning, and if, when I did the self-180, there happened to be a stranger walking next to me, I would all at once be staring at him, and he at me, and our faces would stay uncomfortably mirrored like that the whole length of the street until I turned the corner with a triple pirouette. There were also outbursts of certain jigs; Irish heel clicks; backwards running, skipping; charging uphill with warrior cry. One day I wore all banana-yellow. When I did a yellow-heel click by a basketball court in Harlem, a bench of old men sung out to me, "You enjoin' yourself!" and another bench chorused, "Yeah she enjoin' herself!" I was encouraged. Maybe I was enjoying what they said, *myself.*

However it appears, running backwards in banana-yellow is no joke. I was not doing it for kicks. I was trying to be ridiculous and random to beat the universe at its own game. I couldn't see any reason. No reason for anything at all. Every so often this happens, and it shuts me down, sheet draped over my face, another over the world. Everyday circumstances begin to take on the feel of a familiar word repeated until it disarticulates into some loose mass of senseless sounds. I have to dub simple narratives onto each moment to keep myself grounded. Right now I am staring at my closet door. I am. Staring. My. Closet door. Now. This is my closet door. This is me. Now. Staring at. And so on, in circles. Common objects I usually handle without a second thought—phone charger, bath towel, a pencil—take on an alien shape of flat disconnect. Total irreality. I know it will pass. But I don't believe what I know while I'm in it. There is no time-proven fool-proof way out of this; the solution is a process. Or a virus, constantly anticipating and adapting beyond my next move. A problem is never an object; it's an interface. That is why I keep my eyes and ears open. Which is maybe why I heard the plants. Why I'm yet straining to hear them, from all angles.

And when I hear nothing, nothing from plants, from stories, from people, from waking up, from eating food, from running headlong into the rain—nothing from all the things I usually call life—it's why I would walk backwards. "You know what you need?" said a friend when I wasn't feeling much. "What you need is to throw yourself some curveballs. Eat garlic in the shower." I do. It feels something like new. But give it a couple weeks and backwards and inverse and reverse feel tired.

I call my friend. "I'm doing curveballs," I say, "but maybe I'm tired of being the pitcher." Yes, that's it. I'm tired of the spin coming from me. I want to be on the receiving end. To have force fly into me from without. To hold the out-there fast in my hands. Not long after, I come upon some out-of-the-way lines of Rilke while reading a book on plant poisons and remedies:

Catching things you've thrown yourself
is merely clever or venial profiteering—
it's only when, quite suddenly, you catch the ball
that she, your eternal teammate,
has thrown to your very center,
masterfully and precisely, in a high arc
(like that God would use if building a bridge):

only then is your catching-skill true treasure—
not your own, but the world's...

I take it as a catch.

Despite the handsome serendipity of the ayahuasca equinox ceremony, I said, "No, I can't come," to Michael and then again to the Shaman. Michael asked me to talk to the Shaman one more time. He would answer my questions. I was troubled by the fact that the Shaman said we wouldn't experience nausea or vomiting. I'm not (only) a masochist. From what I understood the physical taxation was an important part of the psychological journey. If I wanted to simply feel good I could take other drugs. The Shaman answered that he used to follow the pain-way of learning, and that it has its value, but that it's ok to learn through love, too, you know? I insisted I couldn't come. "I'm not looking for love. I want the plant to talk to me." Here I laughed in order to temper the possible kookiness of what I'd just said, then realized there was no need with this man. He laughed, but not at me. "Sure, the plant will talk, if you want. But really the medicine is you. You're just drinking you." I hate talking on the phone, and couldn't believe I'd entertained multiple calls in one day with a stranger. I told him I'd sleep on it.

What do you want? I asked myself lying on my back. This question surprised me. What could be more self-evident than want? I want a tree to tell me what it's about. No, what do you want? I want to be spoken to, really spoken to, from another world. What do you want? I want to know what's outside my own head. What do you want? I want to know who I am. What an absurd thing to ask, even of yourself. What do you want? I want to know who I am.

Ok, you heard what he said. Drink yourself.

When the Shaman finally pours the murk red juice into the little sacramental metal cups and passes them around the circle, he says, "This is 'Grandma.' That's the kind of love she'll give you." He looks at me. "We're honored to have you, a very very young grandma." Now there's something I've not been called. "All of this is just you." I drink it down; I've never tasted anything so bitter.

There had been a window of escape. Hours earlier, waiting for the MIA Shaman, Dave and I played barefoot on the shifting edge of ocean water. So so cold and shocking, as it sucked our toes, dragged the sand out from under our wrinkled sole skin. Then we just watched for a while. I said it felt like the randomness of us being there seemed like enough. If the Shaman never showed. Dave said he just had the same thought.

But the Shaman does show, and Dave and I do take the medicine. We want it. I'm vaguely aware that in the moment we take it we're forfeiting the enoughness. Now the experience has to be something else.

A question is starting in on me. An insistence on higher meaning or a higher power—is it a way of attaining greater awareness of life? Or is it to forgo what's already here and happening for the anticipation of something else? I swallow the question down with the rest of the liquid. No questions tonight, just answers, right? Here on the blanket, I can't wait, I can't wait. The Shaman's taking us through this slow. We'll wait another hour for our second dose. Hunched over my cupful, I can't see the ocean.

How did we get here?

Seeing things as they are. No filters. No buffers. Nothing between you in here and reality out there. Conceptual couriers, get lost. Social conditioning, be damned. Stop being you and just be. And remember, but forget, being is non-being; and apply, but release, practice is non-practice. Welcome to Zen, which is all around us nowhere. Sounds good, I thought, disillusioned with thinking. I'm in, or out, or wherever the hell it is living in emptiness puts one. Buddha, I'm there.

The dissolving of objects

And easing of fixations is peace.
The Buddha never taught
Anyone anything.

The voice in my head would not stop until it made itself the whole world and everything and everyone in it. Why does a head always presume it can speak to any and every situation? Please, let me be, I would say. But my saying added to the chatter. Please, please. I don't mean what I'm seeing, I don't know what I'm speaking.

In seeing things
To be or not to be
Fools fail to see
A world at ease.

Ease, that's what tightly wound gray-matter needs. Negative capability, being with ambiguity without irritation, polarization, inflammation. Without rhyme. I want it, raw and messy. Unformed. Bloody. Nameless. I'll believe what you say is not a belief: I am not the mind, I am not the body.

When all I do is think about reality
And let awareness undermine itself—
I must stop.

I would call myself a non-self, using non-sense, if that's what it took to know what in the blazes is going on. I sorely needed a new story to shut up the old ones. And a non-story sounded better than anything I could cook up.

Who creates a creature
Who creates other creatures.
Acts I perform are creatures
Who create others.

On a mound of blankets on a fog-hemmed beach a block away

from the last stop on the Subway the Shaman is saying that it's all a story. He calls it "consciousness play," a term he picked up from a guru with a name as long as this night, unrolling in a mumble and scramble of subcontinental vowels. The face of a man who has been on this earth for some 1800 years is on a medallion around the Shaman's neck. Sometimes it's hard to follow him, accent aside.

Consciousness play can be fun, he's telling us. It's all a story, pick your story. Shake off your stories. Put new ones in their place. It's play! The Shaman told us there would be no nausea. I'm starting to see that this was a story the Shaman told us. Michael's friend next to me moans, "I think I'm going to vomit." The Shaman brightly says, "Why? Do you want to vomit?" But she's already staggered off. Dave and I are lying on our backs side by side. He tells me he's seeing the most outrageous colors and patterns, he never knew his mind could create such colors. I feel nothing but a sudden protest in my stomach. I think I'm going to vomit," is all I can say. The Shaman answers, "Is that the story you're telling yourself?" This is not a story, this is my body, I think, as I crawl over the sand to erupt all this liquid love.

The Shaman, between my bouts of sickness, tells me that this is good, that what I'm actually doing is vomiting up old stories. I'm purifying my sense of reality. I've soiled my shirt. A woolly fog steals in to enshroud our shivering island of blanketed body mass. In here there are no stars, not even an ocean, not even my hands on the ground holding me up as I heave. Bowed down here a fragment comes to me: *Lost in the mists of darkness*. This is a line from *The Book of Mormon*. "Out," I say. Away. I think I must be vomiting this story. I drop back down onto the blanket and wonder what story is already taking its place. I hope not this, not this gray-thickening fiction of non-story.

The next round of purging on my hands and knees, I think, No, I'm vomiting the story of vomiting stories.

How did we get here?

It's popularly said that Zen is not, actually, really, a religion. It's not a philosophy, a doctrine, or a technique. Rather, Zen is pure experience itself—an essential subjectivity which utterly, totally, transcends thought, culture, history, and language. While intellectual thought is caught slug-like in its hardening accretions of ideas, Zen is the light touch that realizes life as it is.

Yet, in life as it is, nothing ever could be that. No system—not even one that negates system—can exist apart from the context that created it. In the case of Zen as we know it, the tradition is a relative newcomer. It wasn't introduced to the West until the late 19th century. What's most interesting about this late crossover is that, as some argue, it was through its introduction to the West that the tradition came to exist in the first place. Japan was facing new challenges, socially and politically, during a period of intense Westernization and modernization. There was pressure to compete, there was pressure to resist, and serious tension between the two. The scientific method had taken hold of Western civilization. Religion had lost favor; its superstitions, rigid practices and non-logical explanations were an unevolved monkey on the back of forward thinking. Scientists set out in search of a universal language, of a unified theory. Jaded with history and religion, everyone wanted to know, What's really going on here? Old ideas and narratives needed to be purged. The world needed a modern faith.

Buddhism at this time was seen by Japanese leaders as a degenerate practice full of folk bugaboos far from the original essence of the Buddha's teachings. A project was undertaken, not unlike those happening in the West, to restore religion to its pure origins. The result would come to be know as the New Buddhism, which proposed to be modern, cosmopolitan, humanistic, and socially responsible. Being formed by Japanese scholars and internationally-minded intellectuals, the blueprint was in no small part based on modern Western thought and technology.

Buddhism did not have a concept for pure experience. This it got from the West. *Experience*, we say, we want. *Ex* should have been the first tipoff that what we say doesn't mean what we want. "A coming forth from." Such a thing won't simply come to you—*ex* is the lexical equivalent of a labor pain. It wouldn't be until the 18th and 19th centuries that *experience* would start to insist passivity, to deny begetting altogether. It was with this new sense of the word that the tradition of a specifically "religious experience" first emerged. Religious apologists proselytized that spirituality and art were in fact after the same thing: truth beyond ideology—unfiltered feeling, spontaneous insight. Of course there had always been religious experiences, but these were a byproduct, an aside, of religion, not its grounds and its aims. Religious experience as supreme and primal allowed a democratic leveling of access to the holy. Anyone, conceivably, could encounter God—it was a matter of inner experience, not outward ritual.

The context that would help to develop Zen is also the one in which Mormonism arose. In the Spring of 1805 a farm boy went and had himself an experience while in an attitude of prayer. He told others to go and have the same, by which they could know personally that what he said was true. The new religion would have personal experience as the authority. Who can dispute what is lived? Experience is what it is. Unless you're thinking in terms of history.

This plant is not working. "Don't worry," is the Shaman's mantra. "Easy peasy," he keeps saying, with a sing-song glee. When Michael asks where his accent's from, the Shaman answers "The planet of love." Michael says, "That's a good one, man! I'm gonna have to use that." But I really want to know. The Shaman allows that he's Hungarian. Also Polish. But that in reality he's just from love, like me, like all of us here, pure love.

I tell myself, it's ok, it's ok to come from someplace messy that was never neat. Having a belly button is not an insult to one's integrity.

How did we get here?

God was my youthful drug of choice. I've heard descriptions of the euphoria and hard fall of heroin that uncannily resemble the experience of my girlhood prayers. Curiously, I never had that experience when I tried heroin. I never felt anything out of the ordinary when I took ecstasy. My non-experiences of these drugs baffled others and greatly frustrated me. Drugs would always seem modest in comparison to my mutterings in pajamas at my long ago bedside.

A very spiritual girl, my parents would say. This, I would come to realize, was a euphemism. Once, my Mom, shaken awake in the middle of the night to hear my exuberant account of a message from God, would unguardedly say, "You're acting crazy." It's touchy talking about talking to God, even—or especially—among those who believe in God, who is, by any other name, a certain way of thinking and talking. Personal visions unsettle the narrative.

It wasn't long after I learned to count past one-hundred that I started telling my mom that I wasn't meant to be in this world. I cried some, on the bottom bunk I shared with my older sister, and I started sticking my fingers in electric sockets, my butter knife in toasters, daring them to beam me to a different realm. I wanted to die the same way I wanted to change out of my stiff school clothes. A matter of feeling free. Fortunately I didn't understand the realities of electric conduction—my poking around was innocuous. Looking at those behaviors it would be natural to infer that I was a sad kid. But I wasn't sad, and not especially angry. Something more like hungry. I wanted what no finger could point to. Fantasy books did or didn't help. Narnia seemed to be my biological planet whence I was trans-existentially adopted. There came a night that this feeling reached an unbearable pitch, which was the only register God seemed to hear, like Lassie, or Flipper. We talked. Our conversation about the problem would become a core story of my personal mythology.

A prayer: Dear God, this world doesn't feel like home. And heaven sounds lame. What's the point of living or even being saved if there's no Narnia?

Here's where, according to the palimpsest of memory,

I suddenly enter into one of my life's most emotionally vivid landscapes, reaching the heights of exact language without words, colors without names, sensations beyond stimulation, all behind closed eyelids. I am transported to a world of unknown feeling, and God says, in essence, "Girl you ain't seen nothing yet."

In my fourth-grade class I had a girlfriend who also loved Narnia. We would talk about the sadness of finishing all the books. So, at the point in a birthday slumber party when she and I found ourselves off on our own, slurping blue Otter Pops on the back deck and fireflies here and there, I thought I'd tell her the vision God gave me so that she wouldn't have to worry about finishing books anymore. I knew, the second the story came out of me, that I was ridiculous. We quickly and silently rejoined the party, and I really knew. Not long after, Mom took the fantasy books away, said I couldn't read them for a while, because they got me too caught up. She was probably right to do it, but I wonder if she need have bothered. I wonder if my friend need have been silent. The fantasy novels would have been traded for more serious books soon enough. The visions would abandon me soon enough. Soon, like a good person, I would not be crazy, just sad. I would do pills, not prayers, but I would never again see all that I saw when childish faith wasn't a sin.

That is, until last spring, when I abruptly woke up to plants. When I woke up to plants awake to me. And life was enchanted again. Too wild not to be true.

"What are you seeing?" I ask Dave. "The colors still, but less. Some wild patterns. And a body rush." "But does your mind feel different?" I press. Dave says it doesn't. He asks if there's anything happening for me yet. I say no. He tells me there's still time. It's about 5 am at this point. If there were magic, it would already be wearing off. Some of our people have wandered off having their inner experiences. Michael's friend is roaming about in a blanket sobbing and telling her awakenings to anyone who will listen. The cute couple, it turns out, is not a couple. She has a nice place in Midtown. He lives on the street. Their connection isn't clear.

The absolute fog has become a sort of lukewarm nightmare to me. I would take terrors, demons, blood, over this colorlessness. I can't look anymore at nothing. I close my eyes and try to conjure my own color show. Vague darkness. There's no manufacturing any convincing color on the backs of my lids and I start to question if I ever could. Inside me, the graying glare of waves and sand in the dark. Dave says it first, "This is sad."

I have to sit up. "You feeling it here?" the Shaman asks me pointing to his chest, patting his heart. "I don't feel anything," I tell him. But I know he can't take me seriously because now I'm crying. "Awesome, perfect," he says. "This is great."

No, Mr. Shaman, this is totally not awesome. This is cosmically shitty. The Shaman keeps repeating that this experience is me, is my mind, is what I'm made of, the story I'm making.

What does that make me? Colorless. Empty. Lifeless...

Stop! I tell myself, but I can't stop crying and the Shaman can't stop saying how beautiful this is. So my insight is that there is no insight? No anything? Not even a blue or a green for God's sake! "Maybe," enthuses the Shaman. Isn't it wonderful! That you were already that perfect?

Perfectly void? I'm devastated. He says I can drink more if I want. I want. I take two more cups, two more than the others. An hour later, when nothing happens, the Shaman taps my forehead and says, "This is what we call ayahuasca hardheadedness." But all I wanted was to get *out* of my head, I protest in my mind. I wanted the plant to talk to me in its own way—why else would I be here? I want. I want.

Here we are. I'm looking around in the gray. A new character has joined us, out of thick air. He has brought his own liquid love, and poncho. His dreads reach his bum; it becomes apparent that he's homeless, as are, it turns out, a few others of our elite consciousness party. He's also brought honey in a jar. Our Shaman is not pleased. "Well that's *one* school of thought," he mumbles under his breath. But aren't schools and thoughts just stories? Soon there is an argument between the honey man and the Shaman about the true nature of honey and its ethical place in the human diet. Even with the wind and ocean the honey man is loud. "Look, what's pollen? What's pollen?" He's not asking. "It's flower semen. Flower semen. You gonna tell me eating semen is unethical?" I turn my head to bury an ear in sand. The Shaman is now wearing a gold plastic and velvet crown. When I look at Dave his eyes are open. He says, "This is how I imagine Hell."

The light hasn't quite come up, but we're not staying. Dave and I shake out the sand as best we can from our many folds, drop our wadded hundred dollars in the Shaman's velvet top hat, then turn to hightail it to the train station. The Shaman is disappointed we're leaving the "cuddle puddle" before sunrise. As we inch away he is slurring a long string of things to me, his crown now drooped to one side and bending his ear, but I'm not listening, hardly hearing, as the waves and fog swallow up the island of misfit consciousness.

Waiting for a train on the platform, Dave and I are seated side by side staring straight ahead in this place that is nowhere we should be at this hour on a Monday night in this weather—or this lifetime. Even the platform and the sign above the platform and the gum smudged onto the platform are gray and graying in the fog. I laugh, I'm laughing. Dave is laughing, too. We keep staring ahead of us at the empty tracks and the laughter is a pinball between our jerking ribs. Dave hands me a granola bar. I take a bite, two, then let it drop from my hands as I race for the garbage bin. The few people waiting for the train move away from me. I heave and heave. Dave moves to stand in front of me. I'm glad I was delusional enough to think inviting him to this experience would help him out.

Once we're underground, that's when I close my eyes, and that's when I find I have an audience with someone who can only be me. Yet it's something other than the daily head chatter of the self. Myself diabolically splits into two competing voices, which are themselves the infinite voices of every thought and narrative I've ever imbibed. My head is hostility with a forked tongue and skinned ears. Each voice only gets a few words before the other cuts it off. But few is too much when each word is a personal shorthand, representing worlds of instantaneous contradictions.

Me: So you did it.

Me: Oh a voice—now you show up.

Me: I was always here.

Me: Don't give me that Shamanic bullshit. You're a sham.

Me: Don't revert to dualities of truth and lie.

Me: Don't deny the reality we live in.

I open my eyes and instantly there are people sitting across from me and I am only one person again. "You Ok?" asks Dave. "I'm tripping," I say. "But only when I shut my eyes." "Oh yeah? What's happening?" I close my eyes again.

Me: You—

Open them quick. It's terrible in that place. I tell Dave, It's like being just me without end. Like I'm being cornered by the very me I was trying to get around. I take in the people seated across from me. When my eyes shut, the me rips them out like a page.

Me: You can't just tear out people! Like they're not real. (Mind flips back to page with people.)

Me: You're still attached to the story. (Tears out page.)

Me: It's not only ever a story!

Me: (Flips infinite pages.)

Eyes open. "See anything interesting?" Dave asks. I don't see things so much as hear their ripping, hear myself talking without stopping in a language of pure undercuts. I'm directing myself to Dave when I say, "There was never any plant goddess who was going to talk to me. It was always just my own brain." I laugh, like it's one big joke. Dave, who knows it never was for me, rubs my back as my head sinks down between my knees. Lady Ayahuasca is a meta-Frankenstein of my most private hell. Maybe this means something?

I don't wait to find out. Before the train hits my stop, I choose to forgo the experience: I open my eyes. I walk out in the early morning light, the concrete sidewalk is gray, and the cement buildings, and the trash blowing around and the drab coats pushing by, all gray. But at least my eyes are open.

I get back to my apartment and the first thing I do is so damn ridiculous to me I cringe as I'm doing it, but I'm hurting, and making sense won't make it stop: I move my three ferns and my purpling echeveria outside of my room and shut the door on them. They're in plant time-out.

Back in my room I curl in a ball on my side. My eyes fall on my bookshelves. There they settle on a maroon leather-bound book with gold lettering, and a good bit of time passes before I pick myself up and take the book in my hands and let it fall open. Mormon scripture. The margins peopled with notes in different penmanship from differing selves. My own history book. It's been a while. I read mindlessly, taking in the familiar words and spaces and cadence—a familiarity that's pained me at times. But on this particular morning, it will be the only thing that can comfort me. Not because it's true. That's not the question right now. It's not what's at stake. It's ok to come from someplace messy that was never neat.

A dialogue from the train runs through my mind.

Me: You're my experience?

Me: I'm your experience of no experience.

Me: What about generosity? Let something be. Not because it's real, but because you feel for it.

Me: That's illusion!

Me: Where does this end?

Me: You tell me.

Ef Why

fecundityfecundityfecundityfecundityf
ecundityfecundityfecundityfecundityfe
cundityfecundityfecundityfecundityfec
undityfecundityfecundityfecundityfecu
ndityfecundityfecundityfecundityfecun
dityfecundityfecundityfecundityfecund
ityfecundityfecundityfecundityfecundi
tyfecundityfecundityfecundityfecundit
yfecundityfecundityfecundityfecundity
fytidnucefytidnucefytidnucefytidnucef
efytidnucefytidnucefytidnucefytidnuce
cefytidnucefytidnucefytidnucefytidnuc
ucefytidnucefytidnucefytidnucefytidnu
nucefytidnucefytidnucefytidnucefytidn
dnucefytidnucefytidnucefytidnucefytid
idnucefytidnucefytidnucefytidnucefyti
tidnucefytidnucefytidnucefytidnucefyt
ytidnucefytidnucefytidnucefytidnucefy

Winter: Welcome When He Goes

In early summer I woke up in bed with a spanking new brain. I had just come back to Arizona from Utah, a land where spring is too chicken to push back against the snow. For months there it seemed that winter would not, in fact, end, ever. Who knew hardly an hour flight was enough to land me on a different planet of worldview. That first morning woke me with light. I rolled over in bed, breathed, eyed, flexed, and so impacted the space of the room, the whorl of the sheets, the very squibs of the air, and when I stood, a sea of particles parted and we were all every bit a phenomenon. I went on my way, making it. I found myself walking outside to some local supermarket.

Summer. Heat streamed from pavement, steamed my bare legs, backs of knees sweat-beaded. When I stepped off the sidewalk the ground gave to receive my weight. Grass, green. It made me come up short. That sweet hushed way it takes you by the feet. Already I was blubbering. Everything means! The world is obscene with meaning, clear as day and dense as dirt!

More than a mood, it felt like a head transplant. It felt like I recognized the world for the first time. And there was this. I didn't want to die. Living didn't feel like a choice I was making. I was just alive, and I didn't question it.

A cool licking blast through the sliding glass doors. When the brilliant colors from the cereal aisle hit me, I secretly wept for the miracle of Cap'n Crunch orange, Raisin Bran purple and gold, glazed infinities of Cheerios. The space between me and suburban ladies pushing shopping carts dissolved and I loved them and our lives. You are a person!

Everywhere, sunlight devolved me to a moony-mush of emotions.

As if my mind interpreted summer like art. What happens to your eyes before art? You think shape, color, context, you think along and in and around, and above all, purpose. Because art has full permission to mean. The reason the fixed eyes of a flat painting can follow you while those of a statue cannot is imaginative complicity: you agree to perceive the flat as three-dimensional. You agree to the art. My body was agreeing.

Before had been winter. Winter surfaces like a funhouse of mirrors. Where where I was was distortion. All was a troubling doubling reflection of yourself, yourself a reflection of where you were, where you were never to find a way out.

But the earth tilts and turns, and shifts happen. I inhabited summer, and the mirrors opened out like windows.

+

The therapeutic effects of light have been noted for millennia. King Hammurabi, in 4000 BC, ordered his priests to use sunlight in the treatment of illnesses. Sun-gardens were kept by the ancient Egyptians, Babylonians and Assyrians. Sunlight in itself was understood to be a remedy for what was called gloom, melancholia, lethargics. Hippocrates prescribed it. A Roman physician recommended patients live in rooms full of light. The Germanic tribes toted their sick to sunny slopes in the springtime to give them their skyfull of medicine. But the sun's position is always changing in the human cosmos. Sun-bathing, seen as a heathen practice, was squelched with the rise of The Church, and so powerful plasma was thrown out with the pagan bathwater.

But you can't keep the sun from rising. The fact that light carries weight when it comes to our psyche was not lost on people in polar extremities. Victorian arctic explorers described a syndrome of fatigue and depressed mood driven by winter darkness. Frederick Cook, an American physician and the first man to reach the North Pole, called it a "progressive depression." In the Antarctic in 1898, his boat thoroughly trapped in ice, he used bright lights to treat the melancholy of his crew. Around the same time there was Emily Dickinson writing about that certain slant of light, the one that oppresses winter afternoons. Yet outside the extremes of ice floes and poetical flow, the connection between sunlight and psyche was not treated as material.

Only in the last three decades has winter gloom been exhumed from its benighted state and remade as Seasonal Affective Disorder, or its darkly cute acronym, SAD. The disorder is characterized by an annual episode of depression usually during the winter and a remission or mild mania in the summer. With the onset of the cold months, mood-boosting neurotransmitters are significantly less fired up. People feel unmotivated, unfocused. They just want to eat. And sleep. And not feel so down. SAD is said to affect 2-5% of the general population in temperate weathers, and seems to increase with latitude, though the relationship between incidence and latitude isn't exactly tidy. For instance, Icelanders, living at intrepid latitude, show a 3.6% incidence, in contrast to the 7.6% among Americans living in lower and greener pastures. Sweden is a saturnine planet apart, with a SAD population estimated at 20%.

It was the Swedes, in fact, who inspired what some claim to be the proto-diagnosis of seasonal affective disorder. Found in Jordane's *Gotica*, the account, written in about 550 AD, gives a history of the Adogit people of Scandinavia. The author describes a 40-day period of continual light in summer and 40 days of unbroken darkness in winter: "By this alternation of sorrow and joy they are like no other race in their sufferings and blessings." While some find in this description the root of what we now know about lack of sunlight and biochemical imbalances, the conclusions reached by *Gotica* and those of modern science couldn't be more at odds. Extreme "sufferings and blessings" cast a very different light on seasons than "transient depression" and "hypomania." In *Gotica*, the earth-spinning intensities of emotional life are seen not as deviation from the norm but as a clarified expression of our humanity, of our emotional inter-relationality. We're given a picture of how emotions create each other, as seasons do: summer highs bloom from winter compost. The shittier the compost, the richer the yield. Whereas with SAD-thinking, seasons become islands, and emotions isolated. For the modern world is not round but specialized.

Though SAD has flooded popular culture, its validity in the scientific community is still hot-and-coldly debated. There are some who dismiss it altogether. They argue that these "seasonal depressives" might just be recurrent depressives who feel crummier in the winter. Others challenge its very existence with a suck-it-up logic. Most everyone gets a little slower, a little pudgier, and a whole lot less jazzed when it's cold and dark out. It's the natural cycle, not a sinister sickness. What's wrong with slowing down and entering a period of contemplation and reserve? Even as my own experiences tell me to ultimately agree with this steely seasonality—that seasons have been shapers of our biology and behaviors since the dawn of life: midwife to form, husbandman of change, forcing life to think again, to think it different, to surrender to discomfort, in ourselves, in the world, and to find we're not left comfortless, that leaves are the underside of returns, seasons teaching us morals in the mud, law of the harvest, principle of rebirth, eminence of impermanence, ever numbered days, and everything in its own time, that these seasons made life as we know it and are making life we've not yet imagined, that they demand blood and give rain, fatten us, flatten us, slick, nip and burn till we bow, pray, dig, kill, sleep, change our ways, cycle back, read the signs, recall the past, forecast, prophesy, ferment, tell tales, chart and calculate and alter and erase, dance like life depended on it, like life is for the upending, and we must keep on, let go, get a grip, grit our teeth, grind together our bodies till babies come in a wave of thaw, and we're all raw, we're depleted, we refresh, and we do it all again, but deeper, quieter, polishing some inward grain, and this is how seasons become us and we become seasoned humans, citizens of the earth, givers and takers and knowers of what we're made of, all balanced on that freaky 23-degree tilt and its psychical slant and cyclical bent and savage arc of empathy—even as my experiences force me to say all this, they also make me shiver inwardly and eat my words.

The truth is, I see no more sense in neutralizing seasons than in pathologizing them. Saying that the ways seasons make us feel are normal may put a stop to the clinical insults, but it doesn't do them justice either. Because natural is lightyears from normal: the earth is a freak to the core. And nature is no tree hugger. She bites.

+

Emily Dickinson, with her deceptively childlike beat, never shied away from joining in the seasonal lunacy. She made calendar a mentality, a space in which self and the world are inseparable. Her poems pull nature up by the roots. She describes Autumn by resurrecting June: "There is a June when Corn is cut/ And roses in the Seed –/ A Summer briefer than the first/ But tenderer indeed." Such lines harrow the rows of linear time, creating psychical time. What she crafted through her work was nothing less than a personal mythology of the seasons.

Thoreau, for all his naturalism, was likewise making myths. He mucked about in seasons believing they held what he called a "solid bottom." They composed the grounds of being, of our being. Today we talk of how our superstitious ancestors made up myths and legends and rituals and festivals to explain the seasons they could not understand. Since we know the facts, we don't need to enact myth. Or is this an ironic case of naiveté? Creating a personal cosmos has gone out of fashion in the face of hard information. We live aseasonally, in the biological darkness of artificial lighting. We are secular earthlings. Where seasons once challenged us to create the personal myths that would sustain and inspire us, they now stand as an arbitrary backdrop for our schedules. Yet there are setbacks to living linearly: We're SAD. So we minimize seasons even more, in a sort of bloodless cycle. Maybe myth doesn't explain the reason behind seasons. Maybe seasons explain the reason behind myth.

When I hear that all eukaryotic organisms—from flowers to birds to the whole of humanity—are descended from a single ancestral population, I impute, but I don't feel, what that means. What I do feel is fresh wonder at all the talking animals, animal-headed persons, and animated soil and rock and tree of ancient mythology. They understood ecological reality: our boundaries are misty, our matter amorously entangled with the *altogether elsewhere*. This is not a sense instilled by insulated walls, filtered light, and processed air, where moderns spend 90% of each day. What in a cubicle suggests that the universe is related rather than random, expanding not contracting? What blinking, beeping contraption is going to sound the gong in me of kinship? Science tells us, all 59 elements in the human body are found on the earth's crust; a story says, from a handful of dust man was made and man shall return. But it's when I stick my fingers in the breathy soil after a good rain that I believe.

I am going to tell you something that a season told me quite privately. It was early fall in a park in Harlem. Summer had burned itself up inside of me and with the change of the leaves a pulse-raising quiet was starting in. The alert calm of Autumn that comes of knowing it's a dying cause. And it's for this reason that I am slowed to a linger: I inhale deep, exhale long; I take the roundabout way home. Happiness is mine when shoelaces come untied and I can bend to the ground, stay a minute, knuckles cozied in the grass. Most of all, I look up. Leaves are hurtling stained glass. Backlit reds and yellows, black purple, pale green. And this is where it happens. I'm brought up short by a cottonwood. The narrow path I'm on is lined by tall sprawling trees on both sides, giving a vaulted cocoon-like feel. Noon, no one else. Light filters through the roundish leaves, and at once they all shiver, all those silvery greens twirling in place, and it goes straight to my head, down into my chest, my blood is a herd, and for reasons more than I can say or begin to know, my whole body is stampeded with tenderness. A feeling something like purity, in the sense that it's love without plans or future or hope, just joy that the tree should exist. Which purity quickly goes to pot when the next feeling tears through: I'm the only one who saw. I'm alone, I'm in love, and it can't possibly be shared. A hurt as unplumbable as the high. That life forces you to know it singly. I can feel myself come apart. *No one's here*. And now, another turn: As soon as I think this, a voice, very still, says: *But I'm here.*

When a voice in your own head takes you by surprise, you have a decision to make. Take it to heart or shrug it off. The force of subtlety is that it won't let you remain passive. Subtlety bids, and you raise it or fold. Life is so much more interesting when I raise. And the graceful recklessness of falling leaves compels me. So it is, October, and I'm given to granting scanty scraps the distinction of dropped breadcrumbs. This small phrase—*But I'm here*—has come to be an enchanted footpath for me.

But I'm here. What a thing to say! Who's here? Spirit? Me? *The tree?* These are live questions the seasons turn up or down, but always touch. On days with good light, it's all three speaking, and inseparably. Months later, after the fall passed and everything was January deep in winter, a friend shared with me a line of sobering advice that she'd been given years before: You will always be alone in the forest. In a rush my head went to standing below that cottonwood. I think I'm alone in the forest. But the trees themselves make this impossible.

Walking home in the cold that night, through that same park, I looked at the weird, twistily textured bodies of the trees and said aloud over and over with wooly breath: You'll always be alone in the forest—and each time, like an old spiritual, answered my own voice—*But I'm here*. Here started my winter mantra. Two lines making a live duet in the dark.

+

To a plant, cold is not the lack of warmth and dark is not the absence of light. Cold and dark are powers in their own right.

While we most often associate plant life and growth with the sunshine, in actuality it is darkness that animates the growth process. Farmers have long observed that crops like corn and sorghum grow taller at night. While most of us assume that plants grow at a slow and steady rate throughout the 24-hour cycle, Charles Darwin, more than a century ago, noted the nightly spurts of plants. Plant stems, he recorded, elongate fastest just before the dawn. These observations, largely ignored in his day, are now the stuff of a continually mystifying truth: plants grow rhythmically, and in this dance, the darkness leads.

In fact, many plants can't bloom in the spring without first undergoing a prolonged period of cold and dark. This is a fertile fact my sun-flung self takes pains to keep in the pocket of her winter coat. The ritual is called vernalization, which stems from the Latin "vernus": of the spring. A misnomer maybe, as the flower actually owes its thrust not to the spring but to the winter— but we humans are remote animals who see only the bright result. The plant's perception of extended cold and dark enables it to distinguish spring from mere warm fluctuations in the fall. Without winter there is physically no spring for the vernal plant. Deep darkness prepares it to recognize the right light, as immersive cold protects it against deceptive warm spells. Vernalization in itself does not induce blooming—rather, it makes the plant capable of flowering when it perceives an opportunity. The plant effectively "remembers" the cold period, then the lengthening days invite it to choose: to bloom or not to bloom.

+

By simply fiddling with light switches we can fool animals into thinking it's summer in winter, or get birds flying the wrong way, or plants to grow wildly out of season. You can't do that with humans. The same lab tests fail to flip our switches. Human beings, we concluded, have evolved past the animal dependence on light signals. Our intelligence could run circles around the sun.

We get ahead of ourselves. In the early 1980s researchers discovered that humans are as responsive to light as the rest of nature's sublunary lot. As in plants and animals, light is the primary stimulus for regulating our physiological and behavioral rhythms. However, it takes much more light to influence melatonin in humans than is required for some other species. When experiments started exposing human eyes to brighter bulbs, our most basic rhythms lit up. Bright light can do a lot of things. The past thirty-some years have seen it produce therapeutic benefits in patients with depression, sleep disorders, menstrual difficulties, and problems related to jet lag and shift work. While the bone-deep effects of light and dark reveal us to be more vulnerable than we thought, they also show we're more connected to the world than we know.

So what is going through our heads when we see the light? The first thing to know is that eyes are not all about vision. Light enters the eyes and stimulates the retina, from where neural signals zip to the visual centers of the brain, but also to the hypothalamus, a non-visual area. Tucked inside the hypothalamus is what's called our SNC, or "master clock," which is responsible for controlling daily rhythms like sleep, wakefulness, body temperature, and hormonal secretions. As it turns out, we don't just look to see, we look to get synched.

The eyes need light to both project the world and to internalize it. Eyes, those old oracles: through their portals non-visual photic info floods your body and synchs its cycles with the surrounding cosmos. It does this on the level of the cell. Organisms are aggregates of thousands of cellular clocks, all beating among feedback loops, coming together to give us our sense of time. Indeed we have "clock genes," proteins participating in 24-hour loops, and countless receptors that sense light and shake their stuff in time with the higher spheres. Is it any wonder that Prajapati, the progenitor God of Hindu myth, is said to have come into being with Time as an internal organ.

+

Recent studies show that between 60 and 80 percent of SAD sufferers benefit from daily light therapy. They also show that antidepressant medication is equally effective. Equally effective, that is, in suppressing symptoms, but not in sustaining change. More lasting are the unwanted side effects. It's a bit peculiar in the first place that antidepressants are used to treat seasonal affective disorder as it's distinct from depression. Here is where the term "disorder" may be doing us a disservice. We hear the word and already we're anticipating a drug, as if the next line to a song we all know. To every season there is a disorder, turn, turn, turn, and a drug for everything under heaven. "Disorder" contains an entire way of thinking, one which tends to divorce problems from their relationships. Winter gets reduced to a senseless crime perpetrated on side-streets of the body. Darkness, a prank-caller, ringing my pineal gland till daily life comes unglued. Dark Season, the recreational terrorizer.

Re-creational, in fact. I am being undone, remade, and when I call the process a disorder, I am essentially saying that I shouldn't have to put up with this shit. Winter is wronging me. It's making me different, and that's a slight to my rights as a self obsessed with coherence and consistency. I am one person, dammit! I won't be made to feel otherwise. Trees can drop their leaves, vermin can change the color of their coats, but I will not give an inch when it comes to my self-concept. I deserve to feel unswervingly myself. Which is to say, invulnerably happy.

This is mental health.

A growing body of research suggests that psychosocial approaches to therapy work better in the long run (nature's notorious time frame) than biomedical "interventions." Said plainly, getting outdoors works wonders. In Denmark, outdoor work has been used to treat those who struggle during the dark season. Winter horticulture groups are bearing fruit. Another study found that an hour's walk in winter sunlight was as effective as two and a half hours under bright artificial light. There seems to be something uniquely galvanizing about light from the sun. Mankind, after all, adapted to the full range of the solar spectrum. Artificial distortions of that spectrum, argue some, have left our bodies in a state of spectral malnutrition. Our prescribed fear of UV light — America's cult of sunscreens, window shades, state of the art sunglasses and UV-shielding clothes—could actually be doing us harm. The trace amounts of UV radiation in natural daylight are vital for normal cell reproduction. And variances of lighting, given by a sun arcing across the sky, play a role in this process. Even the *angle* at which light enters our eyes effects the body. As we are moved by the low blaze of a sunrise or sunset, so too are our cells.

It's a kind of lunacy to maintain we are beyond environment it also resolves. The key is to step outside and engage its challenges rather than retreat from them behind doors. *How* to engage, without getting your human ass beat, is the question.

+

Emily Dickinson, in one of her letters, referred to nature as "old-fashioned, perhaps a Puritan." She often spoke of herself as a "Puritan," and her flowers as her "Puritan garden." No one could associate her with the rigid dogmas of Christian Puritanism. She meant something else. Nature is old-fashioned in the way it has and gives character. Nature is a discipline. Strict, but bounteous. We become flexible, humble, a bit out of whack, and the wiser for it. Seasonal soft spots keep our hard heads newborn.

Dickinson's winter poems punch with this spirited surrender. One poem shows how Dickinson, affected and infected as she was by the cold and dark, found it in her imagination to speak warmly of winter:

Winter is good—his Hoar Delights
Italic flavor yield—
To Intellects inebriate
With Summer, or the World—

Generic as a Quarry
And hearty—as a Rose—
Invited with Asperity
But welcome when he goes.

This world of a woman who elsewhere wrote that winter was a thief and an enemy could also begin a pocm with Winter is good. To a gardener, "generic" would allude to a genus like a plant— a rich and live source, a quarry. As a person who worked as much with flowers as words, Dickinson knew intimately that without snow and frost perennials cannot produce new growth. A "green" winter is actually the death of a garden. To her, winter's character is *italic* — an emphatic element working on the intellect. A *flavor*. In the last eight words, we're given the whole drama of humanness and winter — the interplay of acceptance and subversion; stoicism and playfulness; the need to let ourselves be ravaged, and the humor to keep from being martyrs. *Invited with / Asperity / But welcome / when he goes*. Yes, and yes. The rich strangeness of Dickinson's voice rests on a winter virtue: it says yes to what negates it.

+

A cold that gets in your bones. It's too bad this expression has lost its bite. Philosophically it's stunning. A cold inside you. Chill teething in your very tissue. Winter as a colonizer. Where other seasons draw you out, winter gets in. Sweat you can wipe from your surfaces. Draft, on the other hand, is trawling in your meaty deep. This is insane. The weather should stay on its side of your skin. Think! A cold in your bones. Winter: an obtuse roommate clanging dishes, slamming doors, fiddling the thermostat—and who is this character anyway?—living in such intimate quarters with you. Wind doubles you over and numbs your idea of what is yours, to the very tips. To say that winter isolates us is not the whole story. It also invades us.

I wouldn't feel a bit bad gagging my winter gloom with medication if it weren't so damn articulate. Winter says some importantly upsetting things. It's not like I feel despondent for no good reason. Winter inspires different and darker questions, so that the mood it makes feels more like a timely conversation than some incoherent rant. Winter will always give me more reasons to despair than to live, and that's a valid side of reality. That's reasonable. There are sicker mentalities than winter's slant on death and illness and impermanence. Like, for instance, the insistence on 24-7 well-being. Seen in earth's shifting light, a permanent smile is laughable.

I'm making winter sound like an edifying misery, I should step back and get real. I should say, I start feeling panic in August about January. This last August, the premonitions of darkness became so real that I relocated to the deep end of a pool to save on Kleenex. The tears and snot would not staunch. Morning to afternoon the best I could do was dunk my head at intervals. I was legitimately, if irrationally, terrified for my life. As crackpot as this sounds now, it felt deadly full of sense then, and I know I'll be given to feel it again. And I'm not alone. Studies show a depressive bump in the general population at the end of August. There's no obvious cause. Outside gives no hint of a chill. Skies are yet blue, trees green. Blooms won't bow out for another bit. The world is in a state of seeming-Ok. But your body has the nerve to feel otherwise. A felt sense disquiets you. The wet walls of your insides pick up on some countercurrent, like a licked finger to the wind. It's the sense of too quiet. The sound of everything stopped growing. It goosebumps the brain. Did you feel that? Earth just turned in her grave.

Why am I driven to the depths of a chlorinated Kleenex? To shiver in advance? Winter wants to kill me. Good-naturedly, but winter always takes it too far. That's winter's way. I get tired of the shadows. All its twilit bullshit. Gets to where I'd rather not play. *At all.* Before I go on, let's operate on the belief that winter needs no curing. Unstable, for the moment, is a precondition and not a "condition." In winter I decide I will die. I am going to end. The idea makes a chilly sort of sense. Dear yearly end of the world: Do I exist? What exists? I'll leave and find out.

Though I now know certain thoughts as seasonal patterns, and can talk some June sense into January's tailspin, getting to this point was a process, and one shot with huge risk. As a young adult I didn't know wanting to die could have something to do with the position of our planet. So I tried for death, and I am indebted to failure. My body is a genius. During the dark seasons of trial and error, it would usher me outside again and again, against my will. My body would say, You can't die inside! Get up. Let's go find a bridge. A lake. There you can end. What happens outside?

For me, an astronomical subtlety: I stop seeing from my head. I see in surround. Under sky, myself as yardstick is snapped in half and thrown to the wind. I start seeing from outside. Ha! My hands are so freaking tiny. Look—I'm just a miniature creature, an awkward, bony heartbeat. Hallelujah! I can't be taken seriously.

Earth puts me in the dark, but the earthling in me knows what to do. It gets me out the door and into the winter that shut me in to begin with. The relentless paradox earth tells over and over: I will kill you. But I am the one who brings you back.

Is not treating winter depression as a disorder naive? If a person submits herself to the rhythms of nature, and mother nature ultimately fails to pull this person out of the seasonal abyss, so that this irreplaceable person succeeds in self-destructing, what then? No one could say that it was a courageous decision not to go on medication. It is clear that the seasons demand not just our acceptance, but our enterprise.

We don't need to get back to some primitive relationship with the seasons to experience their power and healing. It would be dangerous to romanticize the lives of pre-moderns in lock-step with the weather. Death, disease, exposure, starvation, immobilization, all came with the territory. Rather than build a wall between us and the seasons with talk of Disorders, and rather than impulsively tear walls down in a flurry of Idealism, we could approach the relationship as we have since our beginnings on earth—as gardeners. We cultivate. Our technology, our knowledge, could be the best way back to nature. Innovations in design, architecture, biotechnology, can bring our daily lives, neighborhoods, and cities, into closer contact with the seasons—without making life unnecessarily harder. For instance, within the past couple of years a group of Taiwanese researchers were able to engineer trees with bioluminescent leaves. The idea is for these lambent leaves to serve as an alternative to street lamps. Would it really make a difference, walking under the soft glow of a tree rather than a street light? A world of it, I think.

+

There was a spell there when critics were cuckoo for pathologizing Emily Dickinson's life. She's received posthumous diagnoses like honorary degrees. Recent dating of her poems has allowed intense examination of the "periodicity" of her work. Scholars and psychologists have plumbed her expressive extremes for signs of seasonal affective disorder, and, as biographers have long commented on the "the winter within her," it's not surprising that her work follows patterns. I wonder what Dickinson would think of these identifications. During her lifetime, she was diagnosed as having "Nervous Prostration." This seemed to mean much less to her than her own words. In a letter to a friend, she wrote, "Possibly I have—I do not know the Names of Sickness."

The results of these recent studies show that Dickinson's productivity has a distinct seasonality: for a couple consecutive years summer accounted for three times the output of fall and winter combined. A letter written to a friend in November shows her wintering mind: "I thought perhaps that you were dead.... Who is alive? The woods are dead." With everything dead, or assuming the look of death, there's not much to say. However, the pattern is radically disrupted in 1861. Dickinson experiences a "Terror" that seems to turn the seasons on their head. She becomes more productive than ever, and in the winter months. This period of crisis and creativity had such an effect on her that she would remark afterwards, "I made no verse—but—one or two—until this winter." What's clear is that creation doesn't discriminate between despair and joy, cold and warm. Creation has one lowly condition: contrast.

The question of course arises: so if, in general, Dickinson was writing wildly more in the summer and all but dying in the winter, what would her body of work look like today if her SAD had been diagnosed and treated? There could have been hundreds—nay, a thousand!—more poems. But can we separate Dickinson's summer output from her winter input? We can chart out and talk up patterns of productivity, but if seasons tell us anything, it's that creation doesn't happen in the moment it appears. Dickinson, naturally, said it best: "Bloom—is Result."

+

I want to go back to the Utahn snow-stifled spring that began this exploration. The false starts, the taunting cold, merciless frost that thwacked back hope—they made for an eventual release. There came a day in May when I was walking to work and it out-of-the-blue hailed—prickling my skin with cubed vicissitude—and I knew something. Discomfort was not the enemy. Routine was the enemy! Smothered impulse! Fear of appearing weird! I stopped dead on the sidewalk. Looked around. People walking, driving, in straight lines. But when I thought about it, or unthought, the sun and hail made me want to shake my ass and wave my arms at the sky, and spin with my tongue hanging out. I was cutting through the Carl's Jr. parking lot when I made the commitment. No more slinking through the motions. I would move with the weather. I would let the weather move me. My body and brain a yearlong *sukkah* porous to the skies. I gave a free dance show to the burger-eaters behind the glass window. There's living as a person, there's living as a human, and then there's living as a fucking earthling. I would be an earthling.

What I'm saying is what I've come to believe: that longest winter was midwife to my new head. Seasons are somehow continuous with consciousness, not a mere metaphor for phases of life, but physically constitutive of them. Seasons evolve us, as organisms, individuals, societies. And not without that heaping portion of darkness. All seasons are incurably connected. Each summer, the brainchild of its winter.

+

The one thing the biologists and psychologists and poets all seem to agree on is this: There's something unique about spring. Just as the plants can recognize spring warmth from fall warm spells, there is something in us that intrinsically knows the spring from the spring-like. Studies related to cognition and weather have placed our peak mood at 72 degrees. Anything warmer or cooler and our performance as people starts to go downhill. According to this model, we should be feeling as optimal on a toasty fall day as in spring. However, as it turns out, the effect of temperature change is asymmetrical: temperature changes towards cooler weather do not predict higher mood. The researchers concluded that there appears to be "something" singularly spiriting about warm days in the spring. There's 72 degrees, and then there's 72 degrees after a long winter. Dickinson could have told them that. "A Light exists in Spring / Not present on the Year / At any other period." More than a millennia ago another poetess, Izumi Shikibu, expressed the fact of the matter this way:

Even though
these pine trees
keep their original color,
everything green
is different in spring.

If only 72 degrees was all there was to it. I could move to some balmy locale and bury my winter brain in the yard. If only there were no order at work. Nature has her own syntax, and for all our sophistication, we can't seem to talk ourselves around it. Against our very human will, we are on a clock bigger than ourselves.

Paper Atmosphere

This isn't a story. This is stage direction. The circus has come to town. The circus has never left. You are seized by a sense of running away to the circus. Of having always already arrived. You find yourself here. You are seized by the need for the audience to understand. We are each a vanishing point in the circus ring, and each vanishing point is the star performer. That's the hilarious thing about stars. They're all far flung, yet every one the center. Center is to say, the mouth made by sucking distance. You need them to understand. You suck your bottom lip, stare out. Hold a beat. You then go about making an invisible circus ring. Go about this the way you go about life. Where possible, an elephant should be present behind you. Now, tear out this page. With flourish: wrist flick like sharp tooth and fine silk, as fiery as airy—this is the circus, dammit! Tear it out, and then bite off a corner. Spit it back into your palm. Pocket it for later. Balance rest of paper on your head. Like so, disrobe completely. You should not come off as naked, nor nude. You should not come off as anything. This point is important, if they are to understand. Now, call Science to your aid. Remove piece of paper from head and place over beach ball. Science insists: it must be a piece of paper and it must be a beach ball. This is the thin layer of atmosphere separating our Earth from outer space. What keeps the cold black suck of soundless space from clasping our thin little wet skins in its everywhere and nowhere arms? It's this paper balanced on a beach ball. Hold it. Of course you are wearing a clown face. Wear it as you wear life. Clown paint, like atmosphere, is a protective layer. It is also a mask. A mask cannot be to scale because a mask is relative to wearer and viewer. And now! For the grand finale of relativity! Which is also just the pre-show! Pull out that paper scrap from your pocket. Ideally, one edge will be serrated with visible teeth marks. Lay it flat on your palm. Spit on it. Spit on it in the way you're sometimes made to spit out life. Allow some spit to remain dangling from your lip, to remain never reaching the paper. Bend down. Finger the dirt between your feet, within the invisible circus ring. Pinch a bit between your thumb and forefinger. Stand up. Sprinkle dirt on spit on scrap. Mix it around. Immediately crumple up scrap into a ball to contain what's there. This is your layer of skin surrounding your wet soily insides. You should still be holding the layer of atmosphere over the Earth in your other hand. Balance these two balls in your two palms. The air around you, and the space outside it, is everything else. Breathe in. Breathe out. Take a bow.

Another Lattice

This isn't an olive branch. Once I pissed at the base of an old gingko tree, in Central Park, in the dark. Enfolding me was that odor of—what?—faint, female blood and sweet, soft rot of bullet-sized flesh. The female gingko, in fact: fruiting bodies Central Park tried to uproot—no luck. On they go upchucking their stink berries, and I lick up the weird with wet nostrils. As every collarbone and bare wrist knows, the most intoxicating perfumes have a touch of death to them. So there I am. Pissing, displacing dirt with my hot insides. I don't take it for granted. In fact, afterwards, I feel to hug the female gingko. I do. Immediately I'm transported to a tree I hugged forever ago in Jerusalem. I feel, not in words, something like: where does one go to not die? By one I mean this accident of me. I don't mean any of this dramatically. But I do mean a character. This character of me being played by a not-me, how do I help her to choose life and not death? I cry into my piss. This is appearing as a theme for this character. In the morning, I remember I love latkes. Love them in the same way I once kissed the grease off a dropped prayer book in my girlfriend's synagogue. The way I think I dropped it on purpose, just for the kiss. The way, later, as a flat and rootless character, I listened to random songs on YouTube in Hebrew and how they hit all the low, root-gnarled notes of my gut, so sloshy and lost at sea. How I couldn't say what I felt. And how that seemed the best reason to feel it. The way I said, that next day, either this love works out, or I move to Jerusalem. How saying it made me laugh. The love did not work out. What a laugh—I move to Jerusalem. There's no why. Because of the trunks of olive trees. Because I was walking through a field of them at night, that braid of their wood like vascular lattice-work, like the life inside is peering through, and the air heavy with lilac, and on the ground constellations of glass shards winking the moonlight. What could I say? Because the breathy bread here makes me want to roll up inside it. Because fallen breadcrumbs in the street are picked up and placed in high places, because bread is life. Because of "To life." Because of the way desert tongues strike straight at my chest, rattle down the spine, to toss and turn and dream in the pelvic bed—and all of it over and under my head. And who can say what that's about? Because at times I'll just be walking along these stony streets and a monsoon of emotion will take me out, crush me with wonder, creation, attraction, destruction, and I have to do a little bee-stung dance, and I see I'm not the only one. Because of people kissing books and licking honey from corners of pages. And what's to say, when this place makes me want to save my breath for breathing. Because it's more than being happy. It's feeling alive.

Siren Song

Summer is the time to go on holiday, Jerusalemites tell me, because summer is when blood gets hot and war breaks out. The UN has not yet recognized a positive correlation between degrees and missiles, but I feel it on the ground. Jerusalem, on a normal breezy day, is easily ten planets in one. Turn up the sun, and she manifests full-on multiple-cosmos disorder.

For her I sing the needle-skipping song of world hopping. Both feet on summer fire on shifty stones.

+

My mind flashes to this month last summer. I was camped out with a small group of people in the Arizona desert. It was sometime in the night, hardly a moon, a handful of stars, I crawled out of my blanket to go take a leak. The ground was a checkerboard of indigo juniper shadows. While I didn't wander off very far, I found that when I turned back to camp, I was in a different landscape. No. On a different plane. Everything had shifted, rotated. Translated. I saw our fire, but it was not our fire. Where my group had been sleeping on the ground was now a ring of rocks. What was uphill was downhill, what was desert, wooded. There was a cowboy hat on a fence silhouetted against the sky, which was a different sky. For a second, wildfire panic swept through my body. And then it snuffed out, totally. And there in the fear's place, from far inside, came the shrug of all shrugs—a metaphysical one, deep in my mental musculature—that said: *Huh, so I guess here is where I cross over into another dimension. Ok.*

It was the opposite of a psychotic break. It was a psychic homecoming. My twilit mind revealing to me just how deeply I believe in the fundamentally unbelievable nature of this world.

Maybe this is the quality that drew me, an utter outsider—Scandinavian-American agnostic from polygamist Mormon stock, anyone?—to Jerusalem in the first place, and what keeps me here, shockingly at home in the otherness. Jerusalem is my style of reality. Kaleidoscopic, a kind of kinetic montage, divergent worlds and scenes and sounds blurring and colliding and cutting and jumping—where the daily spontaneous catechism is How in the world did I get here?— said with doubt and hope and delight and wonder.

And, lest I fool myself—fear.

+

Worlds killing each other, worlds flattening other worlds, worlds insecurely securing only their world as the world, unchecked worlds of check points, worlds going around, coming around, dark moon worlds you pray under to bring back the light, because it's a world where there's a story that says the sun and the moon used to be equal, that the world is made not of atoms but stories, and stories are shadow phases of the world with power to faze out the Other or give her a face, oh our Father, bless us now with foreign tongues and forgive us our familiar stories.

+

Stay out of the Muslim, Armenian, and Christian quarters, said the security email. So of course I would meet on my night walk an Armenian Palestinian who lives in the Christian quarter. And follow him home. As with most every meeting in Jerusalem, this was not our first. By some cosmic sitcom force, in Jerusalem we are all cameo visitations in one another's lives. You see the same people again and again. And without going into names or places or phone numbers, you fall into conversations like you'd always known each other.

So it was that when he and I bumped heads on Ben Yehuda Street, we were suddenly talking about the modern exile of spiritual masculinity, peace farms in Kentucky, and his neighbor who got the crap beat out of him this week. He doesn't look Palestinian. And he let that fact unfold slowly. Our greeting turned into a walking, turned into journeying, and he told me about hiding his identity as a hormonal teen, trying to get with Israeli girls because what options did he have in his own culture? and how that lie messed him up inside and how later, when asked "what" he was at a check point, he said all pointedly "Palestinian" and how that word messed up his face with bruises. I've heard these stories before. What was different was the Buddha grin he told them with. "Thank you for asking," "Thank you for listening," he kept smiling. His family fleeing genocide in Armenia, then from Turkey, then Syria, then arriving in Palestine, just in time for The Catastrophe. And he was telling me this with kind eye crinkles and no residue of bitterness. "I made it a study," he said, "if you can love your enemies. I wanted to know if it was real. And it is, a scientific fact. I'm not interested in Palestinians or Israelis. I care about humans."

He led me through the Old City gate, into the labyrinth of the Christian quarter, incense-infused and vaguely rotting. I thought it was a bad idea for a whole half second. He unlocked the gate to his home. A vast, moon-soaked courtyard surrounded by stony rooms. A basket sat under the gibbous moon full of ragged soccer balls—"Bombing our courtyard long before the 6 day war." He showed me inside. Spice tea and cushions and Turkish delight, Lebanese music—we were dancing, twirling, clapping, him teaching me traditional steps and me spastically transgressing them—we arm wrestled, we leg wrestled, and from my place as the loser sprawled out on the floor, I listened to him play the Oud and sing Arab poetry. An extra note here and there of gun shots. As I left we told each other our names.

+

If my whimsical ass had been just a few kilometers to the east, I would've heard a different world: fire bombs, noise bombs, tear gas, rock throwing, rioting and chanting, shooting, police, ambulances, not even one love poem.

+

Jerusalem has meaning beyond its means, bursting at the seams with its own symbolism.

There's the feeling that I'm always crossing thresholds. Climbing branches that just keep branching. Now a stranger is barbecuing me lamb, now I'm helping in the kitchen of some church, now I am praying at the Wall, now dancing at a disco, klezmer and protest, absinthe and Zohar. Reading in a park a woman asks if I want to walk her dog with her. A friend and I serendipitously converge on a footpath at midnight under the moon, and the wondrous feeling that nothing could be more natural. This is one day.

What is this rapid-fire metabolizing of reality? I feel like it has something to do with the warmth—and the heat—that is radiated here—by the people, by the stones, by the friction of devotion. You feel it under your skin—the thigh bruises of angels, flowing oil of lovers, rugburn of siblings wrestling from the womb.

+

Before it was confirmed last summer that the Arab boy who died was in fact a revenge killing by Jews in Jerusalem, I was at shabbat dinner with friends. We said a blessing for the families of the kidnapped and murdered Jewish boys. Then one of the guests said, "I think we should say a blessing for the Arabs." He talked about how he'd never been ashamed as an Israeli until the past week. Everyone started talking, mostly talk about why would we want to talk about this? Too heavy for shabbos. And then my friend, and our host, gave over a lovely bit of kabbalah about how we need to engage the dark and muddy to elevate those things to a higher level of consciousness.

With all that talk, we didn't say the blessing for the Arab families.

I found myself very upset later with all the abstractions. Why couldn't we do something concrete and give that blessing? And then I was bolt upright upset at my thought. Since when has prayer been concrete? I've been in Jerusalem too long.

+

Before we knew there were missiles headed to Jerusalem, I was at a forum with a speaker from ACRI, The Association for Civil Rights in Israel. ACRI denounces the Israeli airstrikes in the Gaza Strip that target residential buildings. The Israeli woman speaking worked in East Jerusalem. She told us about the violence and violations she'd seen over the past week between Police and Arab-Israelis. She showed us pictures and stories. She was surprisingly soft-spoken, has family living in Zionist settlements, and shared powerfully disturbing facts. "I love my family, and they love me. We just don't talk about my work." Separated worlds without end.

I left on fire with the Palestinian plight. I met a Zionist friend for dinner, we sat outside and argued.

When the first siren went off. Jesus—what a sound. A ghostly alarm straight from the black and white cinematic abyss of World Wars. It flooded the whole city. What is that? My friend and I looked at each other. People were running, rushing, confused. We followed a panicked crowd inside.

You mean to tell me a missile can reach right where I'm sitting?

Well this was a different story. I wasn't thinking about safe water and electric access for Palestinians anymore. A deeper bias, both perverse and natural, had been born in my intestines at the first howl of that siren.

I get it, that I don't know anything. What living with chronic fear can do to a person and whole peoples.

+

After the sirens we watched the futbol game outside, like always. Small streets of big screens, beers, throngs. In response to the sirens, everyone ordered another round. What else to do? said the girl who insisted we two l'chaim, and l'chaim again. We heard the boom, and another boom.

Nine boys had the same idea to go out and watch the game, in Gaza. The bar blew up, their body parts scattered in the sands.

+

In Jerusalem, sound, too, is a layering of worlds.

Against my writing is a background of traffic. I half-hear the constant stream of car horns, high and low, faint, harsh, when one sound peels off from the noise, rising, hovering over the honking void. My ears perk up and I realize, with a chill, it's a ram's horn. Re-calling that ram in the thicket.

Abraham, don't you touch that boy.

+

A techno song plays in a bar in West Jerusalem. At once I see everyone flinch, look around. Was that a siren? Everyone laughs nervously. It's in the music. There are sirens in the song. Jerusalem, psych of song of songs. Can someone please play something else?

+

On Saturday morning I do not visit the Mormon church, which is on lockdown. But I can't stay away from Jerusalem's flaring innards. I find myself walking around the wall of the Old City. Around inside, and around again outside. My head is covered and my face is veiled, a walking outside-inside. The evening before, before prayers in the synagogue with a curtain between the women and the men, I was outside reading in the grass—my own sacred ritual. A man came to lie there, close by, and I thought, Ok it's a free world, when the man started pushing his hips into the grass digging his eyes into me. And before this, the black-hatted Ultra-Orthodox man who out of the blue kissed my face and ran like hell.

Because in Jerusalem people are such lovers they kiss stones and books and walls and ruins and every alley of the Old City glistens with lip grease, a sliding slipping love, a city loved up unto death, you have to shroud yourself against so much love, and the veils create more desire and the mounting desire creates more veils and all things hurt and destroy in all that holy mounting.

Don't look at me. I don't want your violence. I'll be violent back. Cover myself until I cut you out of sight. That's how I add my violence today, walking Jerusalem above the graves, body and face wrapped up with a scarf and a book, reading inside a gauzy blue womb. And from inside I can read out loud, pronounce a poem over the city.

Why is Jerusalem always two, of above and of below   and I want to live in Jerusalem of in between   without hitting my head above without stubbing my toe below   and why is Jerusalem a pair like hands and legs,   I want to live in one Jerusalem   Because I am only one I and not many I's

But the want of one Jerusalem means one must be many at once. And you can read 'want' both ways. Any way I read this place, I have too many I's to fit in my head. I got no blessing for you Jerusalem but my equivocations. A sacrifice of my first-born stories. A covenant to rethink them, and a commitment to no conclusion.

+

One of Jerusalem's most far-out world-hoppers uses my friend's apartment as his threshold. That's where I met him one evening. My friend got a call, said someone he knew was stopping by. Ok, cool. Then in walks a Haredi man with black beard to his mid-chest, long flowy forelocks, black hat and long black coat. He knew who I was. (World-hopper radar.) But I had yet to meet his other self.

He had us get to work, and play dress-up. Trying different hats on him (black sombrero, lady's sun hat, teardrop fedora), different t-shirts, stylish jackets. He tied his spiraled locks in a knot on top of his head, tucked under a newsboy cap (the winner). And then he was off and running to paint the town not black and white.

I run into him all over the underworld. He appears, rocks out, vanishes again. "There's day and there's night," he said to me, "but you don't say they're separate. They go together. Life is hard, so I figured out a way to live. I don't see a contradiction."

Last week, walking back from the Kotel alone at night, I saw in the yellow glow of an Old City alley a small group of men in traditional silk striped robes, more beard than face, and on their heads those huge furry barrel hats, and one of them was grinning at me. Odd. "*Shalom*," he said, as I passed. I did a double-take. My friend, in his full Haredi glory! We had danced together like space aliens in a Russian bar the last time I'd seen him. Though we couldn't let on, I smiled the whole way home.

Night and day aside, I still want to ask him, *How?*

+

Shabbat afternoon I run into an acquaintance leaning against King David's tower.

"Where you going, *hamuda*," he says. "To the Armenian Church." He gets a shocked look. "I didn't know you worship idols." "I worship The One, babe." And I pinch his cheek. "You don't want to go there, come with me to the park for Shabbos lunch. They're your kind of people." "But I'm going to the Armenian Church." He doesn't smile, says, "Say Hi to those idols for me."

This is a hello? In Jerusalem it is. Hey what do Jerusalem and Halloween have in common? Every greeting starts with Hey what are you.

+

"Then Judaism can go to hell," says my teacher at yeshiva, where they kindly let me play spiritual anthropologist. "I don't worship Judaism. I worship God. And God is what is worthy of service and worship." He is something like a pro-Palestine Zionist, which labels are stupid and ill-fitting on such a vast, textured consciousness as this guy. He believes in Human Rights. And he proves with the Torah that Human Rights Covenants trump Torah, every time. The Messiah comes in robes of species-wide legal norms to protect human beings everywhere. The thing is, he doesn't go looking in Torah to justify his liberal values. He assumes they are already there, because he assumes God has the highest humane values he can conceive of. He doesn't justify God. He assumes God. And that approach to text is enough to rock one's assumptions about having assumptions and grant a nebula-load of permission.

I met Shaiya four months ago, when by twists and turns I ended up in a seat in his Kabbalah class. He welcomed me and warned it was going to be a weird one. I remember him chanting the Aramaic, my skin prickling, as I followed these funky visualizations of God's skull and nose and beard. In His eyes, the sages say, there are three colors: white on white on white. Oh the holy sense of humor. I remember how at the end he said, "Sorry if none of that made any sense for you." And how the tears were already down my neck. In this world where so many facts fill my head and leave me empty, thank god for substantive nonsense. A breeze between lines.

+

A story from the Kabbalah: In the beginning God made the Kings of Edom. They hung around for a few generations, but ended in total failure. So God stretched himself out on a canvas and remade herself. Now God was ready to make Adam in his/her image.

Why, ask the rabbis, were the Kings of Edom a flop? Because, they say, the names of their generations did not include the names of their wives. Something wrong there.

No face-to-face tension = cosmos dead in the water.

Recipe for a universe that survives: It is in conflict with itself; it searches after itself; it cannot satisfy or fulfill itself.

When you read the news, if it lacks the names of the other side, you know the world is dying. That would be the ultimate robust universe, right? ... The one with the names of every relational becoming, the wives and husbands and women and men and girls and boys—of every State and non-State—and when all their flesh and blood and relatives and relativities and unkissed interstices are witnessed, then also the names of the animals, of the trees…

+

My Austrian roommate in West Jerusalem was teaching in East Jerusalem for a time. No matter she's an intelligent, compassionate person, and has the permission of an Outsider to boot. A day came when working in two worlds was too hard. Emotional, spiritual whiplash, and narrative trauma to the head.

I hear this story so much it's a Jerusalem genre. Expansive people commute between worlds. And then one day they go home, shellshocked from incongruent cosmos, and don't come back.

+

There's a tune that hums me low every weekend. Maybe you know it. I call it the Shabbat Blues. It plagued me in America, too, but that was just a shadow of the Shabbat Blues to come. I adore and I dread Shabbat in Jerusalem. It refuses integration. It WILL be set apart. And if you are not a part of the apart, then you're on your own even among the hosts. Inside/outside. I feel the yearning energy, the high, the depths, the words and rhythms and braided bread and blessed wine get down in my body, and I rise up and make to be one…

When I feel my face violently smoosh against the glass, outside looking in. Hell I don't speak this language. I'm not Jewish. I don't know what I am. Human, I'd say, but it sounds a bit thin. In those profound words of true blue rock—*I'm a creep, I don't belong here.* For me Shabbat is not so much a break from the world as a break with it. Another turn to another world, one I'm shut out of and anyways refuse to enter on anyone else's terms. In Jerusalem the Sabbath exists for or against you, and both in turns. It is the formal institution of absence as presence.

+

Ever heard of the Cohen blues? Now that's a tune that will play you! Of course it happened: I fell hard for an Orthodox Jew. We met (unavoidably it seemed) my first week in Jerusalem. Our third date he told me that he can only marry an "originally Jewish girl." And I thought, That works, because I can only marry a not racist person. Of course we kept seeing each other.

"Out of everyone, why the Cohen? It's uncanny. Like is there something deeply masochistic in me that is attracted to whatever keeps me outside? When all I want is home?" Telling my friend this, he laughs. "How Jewish of you. Welcome to the family."

I feel myself becoming at home in my outsiderness. But never at rest. Home like a nucleus of waywardness with positive and negative charges.

+

Separate worlds without end. Or maybe I'm thinking of this wrong, and sad. Maybe I should think not so much parallel lines as origami. Manyfold worlds.

Manyfoldness as a holy gift. The Lord is my shepherd of folds. I lack nothing, including lack and nothing. He makes me to lie down in green fields, quantum fields, gathering into the fold, wormholes, brain folds, paper folded along a loving spine, the love of the folded God in the folds of spacetime for the manifold of becoming, mindful of those not of this known fold, His unfolding must bring them in also.

+

Just down the street from me, this wildman bedouin character,

Isaiah, used to hang around and trip out on visions of a new world order. That was nearly 3 millennia ago. The neighborhood is still trying to catch up.

And it shall come to pass in the last days... many people shall go and say, Come ye, and let us go up to the mountain of the Lord, to the house of the God of Jacob; and he will teach us of his ways, and we will walk in his paths: for out of Zion shall go forth the law, and the word of the Lord from Jerusalem. And he shall judge among the nations, and shall rebuke many people: and they shall beat their swords into plowshares, and their spears into pruninghooks: nation shall not lift up sword against nation, neither shall they learn war any more.

...And after there is peace among humans, this wild visionary brings in the animals, the trees...

The wolf also shall dwell with the lamb, and the leopard shall lie down with the kid; and the calf and the young lion and the fatling together; and a little child shall lead them.... They shall not hurt nor destroy in all my holy mountain: for the earth shall be full of the knowledge of the Lord, as the waters cover the sea.

I fold the corner of the page. It's not enough. Fold it like origami, my hands curled up in it.

Tree, A Triptych

I,

I am not writing you. I'm not seeing things right right now. The way I see it now: I'm walking, the world's a city. This night the cold picks at my eyes like scabs. Streetlights seep into fingerpaint smears: big bubble heads, fat black posts bleared into spindly legs. The shapes they cut look glued onto the night and not part of it. Nothing looks part of anything. I tell me out loud, don't validate the world in your head. Don't word this. I tell myself the city suddenly looks deadly because, any time after dark, bright lights are likely to surface as cancerous flat splotches. I come

I Am

a tree to you. I could be anything, but we both agree *God* is not what we mean. I AM: You fill in the blank. Do I sound like your voice? So speak. You'll have to get over it: I don't see you. I see *with* you. Right now: blobs of scribbled light. You're running with this in your head, running it ragged. You're crying now. And now the lights bleed more. You see degenerate sunspots. The imminent dark in light, death in youth, and so on. What to say. Walk away, let's just walk away from the cop car's gross

A Tree

I knew fell and we're not ones to right ourselves. Leaving me to stand here alone, which you want to mean set apart. I don't blame you. Who I am shows like a sign. Rigid, unable to stretch, my bark shatters and falls, spalls off in jigsaw fragments. Giving the look of something made to be solved. Relax, kid. This mottled trunk is no riddle. Skin must yield to growth. A process we all perform. I just show it more openly than others as I break myself bare. Let it go. A plane tree rises as it drops. But you, you blow back and forth, a graspy rootless thing. Your breadth takes the air out of me. Your bone-potted irises, green with envy, say, me, a tree, is what lives at the heart of it—a spring of immediacy, seamless suchness. Bullshit. What do you from desert women. The sunspots covering the hands of my grandma like sepia-lace gloves, and the galaxy-dense blotches populating my mother's back— these would repulse me as a girl as much as they transfixed me. I would poke a cluster of spots, crinkle my nose and ask, Why 'cause? Because, the women said, I loved the sun too much as a girl. This perplexed. That love is a stain in waiting. That sun is a cold exacter. That beauty is a slow-release ugly. Measured by time, light had dark counterpoints. I think now, darkness is what light falls back on when it runs out of things to say. Tonight there's no saying what these lights I'm seeing mean.

kind of BLUE, RED. We can just let lights be lights. Nothing has to mean what you think just now, when to think is to begin with maybe, maybe not. I see the tree when you do. White, skyward forking. I know we're in for it. I'm in. I'm with you as you cut across the crackle of winter grass. There, the tree's stiff bark bites into your cheek. Between your nose and its skin is air that has for you a clean and secret scent. You wrap your arms around the trunk and breathe like a tantrum. You say things like *please, please*. What would please you, kid? What would you have me say as god as

think I do all day? Damned if I'm not making my life from the ground up. Yet if I didn't believe the rain falls for me, I'd die of thirst. So go on, believe my presence sees you. You come to me, a little thing. Your beating trunk against mine, your two limbs twined round me. You breathe like rocks tumbling. Your bones shake. I know what this is: vascular sadness. How can I speak to this in language you hear? You're making noise about how you could be wrong about everything. Look up, kid! All waywardness is saying is home exists. Think, your grandma's hands. Cool string beans of her fingers, chapped pods where the bones swell. In her the sun has been it all: rosy to bronze, blemish to stigmata to melanomata. Knowing what light is comes by warping it. By being warped. You refuse tonight. Downcast and blur-eyed, you won't remember: looking

There's a cop car on the unlit park path, siren lights, BLUE,   RED, spray-painting tree trunks and snagging in my lashes. I turn and go the other way. Look and there's a tree like no other! So light it is what it is even at night. I'm not new to it. I pass it everyday. But now it looks like what I've been missing all along. A few steps and I'm hugging the thing like a regular loony. I smell,   touch, taste, say, *please, please*.   But I don't sense a damn thing. I retch. I vomit at its buried feet.   I am not writing   nothing.

the tree as you? I'll say it just as soon as you do. You thought you saw me once in a tree.   So you're back knocking on wood, as if a door. I've seen it before. Moses set himself on fire trying to make   that   bush burn twice. And Jonah,   cradling some   washed-up fish in his palms, *Open up, please, please, open up*. Trees are here, like you are, and everything   else is.   What sign is more than here?

straight   up   and seeing the torqued world of my arms. You sounded off me, *Dendrite. Dendrite*. You shivered, looking at a wooden double of your own brain. You sounded off me, *Dendrite*. Then where is the spark? you pleaded. Where's the shock of a signal? Only dark filled your view. You won't remember how you bent back, arms holding onto me, the rest of you an outshoot to see sky behind you. There: Moon, high. Through the   bramble,   you watched the full jolt of it electrify one of my far-reaching tips. You righted yourself, disgusted. The moon touched   nothing. Connection was all ridiculous   angling on your part. But tell me   sometime,   are we not all bending to make dead ends meet? You're not real, I won't write you real, you   spat   into   the black. And so you won't remember: the way my arms bent to give you a view of moon.

M O N N O M
O O O
M O N O M O O M
O O O O O O
O O O O O
N M O N O M O N
O O O O
N O M M O N

M O N O N M O N

Acknowledgments

Much gratitude to the editors of the following publications where these pieces first appeared:

CounterNarratives: "Treehab"

Dialogue Journal: "The Ecology of Absence"

Gravel: "Trip Down Happy Valley," "²Brood"

GRAVITON: "Found: Zero in Nature"

The Offbeat: "Ef Why"

Split Rock Review: "Eye Sees Yes"

The Swamp: "Piss on Heartsick"

Unbroken: "Paper Atmosphere"

Masque & Spectacle: "Winter: Welcome When He Goes"

Two Cities Review: "Tree, A Triptych"

You Are Here: The Journal of Creative Geography: "Siren Song"

"Dirt Tea" was made into an artist's book on display at Columbia University's Butler Library

About the Author

Brooke Larson is a writer, collagist, and sometimes wilderness guide. She holds an MFA in Creative Writing from Columbia University, and is currently finishing a PhD in English at the University of Louisiana at Lafayette. A chapbook of her poem-plays, "Origami Drama," is forthcoming through Quarterly West.